Preface

2. Da Nang (188~311)

3. Ho Chi Minh City (312~470)

Preface

You will come to realize shortly that you can get all attractions at the 3 key cities of Vietnam by yourself. They are Hanoi, Da Nang and Ho Chi Minh City. In addition to the detailed information especially on the "ways" to the must-visits, maps and photos indicated by arrows and explaining boxes will give you full confidence for your try Vietnam. Only except "Ha Long Bay" and "Ninh Binh", outskirts of Hanoi, you can get all of the hot places by your own self. You need neither to chase after a guide nor ask passers-by for your destination.

This book goes to the northern city of Hanoi first. It is the capital of Vietnam for more than 1,000 years. Emperor Ly Thai To moved its capital from Hoa Lu to "Thang Long" in 1010. "Thang Long" means "Ascending Dragon" and changed its name to "Hanoi". "Ha Long Bay", one of the 7 World Best Landscapes, will be introduced after Hanoi. And, "Ninh Binh", called as a "Ha Long Bay on the Land", is also featured at the finish.

Da Nang, the biggest city in the middle area of Vietnam, will be introduced after Hanoi. In addition to the attractions such as the incredibly long beach of "My Khe" at Da Nang, you will meet "Old Town" at Hoi An, which has been designated as one of the World Heritage by UNESCO.

Ho Chi Minh City, the utmost southern city of Vietnam, will be featured at the finish. You will meet so many beautiful attractions at the economic capital of Vietnam. The gorgeous colonial buildings such as City Hall, Opera House, Notre Dame Cathedral, Central Post Office and Reunification Palace are all accessible on foot.

Even no subway yet, you can pay visits the whole attractions cities by your own self. How to get there and which bus you have to take are all explained in detail through maps and photos. Tour bus will be introduced only for the ways from Hanoi to the outskirts such as "Ha Long Bay" and "Ninh Binh".

Keep this book in your pack and fly to Hanoi, the 1000-year-long capital city of Vietnam. Then, it will cast lights on all the ways to the must-visits of Vietnam.

Hanoi

(Motorbikes, the legend of Vietnam, are running on the wide street of "Dinh Tien Hoang" by the "Lake of Hoan Kiem".)

(One of the 7 World Best Landscapes, "Ha Long Bay".)

Content

1. City Summary

Hanoi is 1000-year-old capital of Vietnam. Its original name was "Thang Long", i.e. 昇 龍 in Chinese. It means "Ascending Dragon" in English. Emperor Ly Thai To moved the capital from Hoa Lu to current Hanoi in 1010. A legend on the name says that he named "Thang Long" after the shape of an ascending dragon flying to the sky from the Red River which is located near Old Quarter of Hanoi. Old Quarter is one of the well-known area to the travelers from all over the world. Vietnam held a giant ceremony in 2010 to celebrate the move of capital to Hanoi 1000 years ago.

Ha Long Bay, one of the most attractive spot in Vietnam, consists of around 2000 islands on the sea. It takes around 4 hours from Hanoi by bus. Ha Long Bay has been designated as World Natural Heritage by UNESCO in 1994 and nominated as one of the 7 World Perspectives in 2011. When "Thang Long" means "Ascending Dragon", Ha Long comes from 下 龍 in Chinese, i.e., "Descending Dragon". The legend on Ha Long Bay says that a sacred dragon flying down from the heaven vomited thousands of magical beads from its mouth against the invaders to Vietnam and the magical beads transformed into the countless islands on the sea after defeat the enemy.

(Hanoi is located on the northern part of Vietnam.)

(1) Currency

Vietnam Dong ("VND") is national currency of Vietnam. They simply say the price with the remains after cut off the last 3 digits on the currency. For example, they say only "500" in case of VND500,000. US$1.00 is around VND20,000 as of July 2015. In that case of VND20,000, you will hear "twenty".

(All monetary notes bear the portrait of Ho Chi Minh.)

(2) Transportation

There is no subway in Hanoi. Therefore, train, bus and taxi would be all for travelers. You can also rent a motorbike, the legend of Vietnam, or you can take cyclo, a carriage run by bicycle. Actually, you can take a full look at the famous Old Quarter on foot. When you go to Ho Chi Minh's Mausoleum Complex, you will take a taxi. For Ha Long Bay, tour bus would be the best.

(Motorbikes are running on the wide street of Dinh Tien Hoang by the legendary Lake Hoan Kiem.)

(3) Language

Signs on the road, announcement on the bus are all serviced only in Vietnamese language. On the other hand, signs at museums, menu at restaurants include French and English. Moreover, staff at hotel and tour guides speak English very well. Therefore, even a stranger at Hanoi, you don't need to worry about the difficulty of language.

(Name of the road on sign are all written only in Vietnamese language. Bus stand and announcement on the bus are also serviced only in Vietnamese. However, airport, monument, temple and restaurants have English signs and menu. Even you may feel a little confused in the beginning, you'll be accustomed shortly. It would be no matter for your wonderful journey in Hanoi.)

(4) Heroes

There often appear 5 heroes in Vietnamese history. You can find many roads named after their names. In the order of history, (a) Emperor Dinh Tien Hoang comes first. He reunified the northern Vietnam for the first time. You will find that one of the most important streets of "Lake Hoan Kiem" is "Dinh Tien Hoang Road". And, (b) Emperor Ly Thai To who moved the capital city of Vietnam from "Hoa Lu" to "Thang Long", current "Hanoi", in 1010. You will meet his statue standing by "Hoan Kiem Lake". (c) The third one is "General Tran Hung Dao" who defeated Mongolian invasion in the 13th century. His statue is standing at a vast rotary by the Saigon River, Ho Chi Minh City. (d) General Le Loi (1385~1433), later King Le Thai To, achieved Vietnamese Independence from China in the 15th century. According to a legend, he used the divine sword which is said to have been delivered by a turtle from Lake Hoan Kiem. After defeat China, he returned the sacred sword to the turtle, they believe. His monument is prepared on the road of "Le Thai To" by Lake Hoan Kiem. (e) President Ho Chi Minh can be the last one. They even changed the name of Saigon into Ho Chi Minh City in the respect of Ho Chi Minh. They call him "Bac Ho (Uncle Ho)" rather than President Ho. He refused to move in Presidential Palace and lived in a humble one-story-house built on stilts since 1958 until he died on the 2nd of September 1969. Presidential Palace at Hanoi has no owner yet. If you come to Ho Chi Minh Museum, you will come to know his name in his youth, "Nguyễn Ái Quốc". Vietnamese people love him so much.

("Emperor Ly Thai To Statue "is standing on a small park by "Lake Hoan Kiem".)

NGUYỄN ÁI QUỐC, NĂM 1924.
Nguyen Ai Quoc en 1924.
Nguyen Ai Quoc in 1924.

(Ho Chi Minh, "Nguyen Ai Quoc", in 1924. He was 34 years old. Good looking.)

2. Public Transportation

As explained earlier, there is no subway in Vietnam now. Only in Ho Chi Minh City, the first line of metro is under construction. Therefore, travelers have to use taxi, bus, motorbike and cyclo.

Airport minibus between Noibai Airport and Lake Hoan Kiem will be introduced first. Noibai Airport is the international airport of Hanoi. And, the free shuttle between Noibai Airport and terminal 1 for domestic flights. Tour bus which is the most convenient transport for the outskirt cities such as Ha Long Bay and Ninh Binh, will be followed.

(1) Airport Minibus, Taxi and Free Shuttle to "Terminal 1" for domestic air flights.

Travelers usually book a hotel at Old Quarter which consists of 36 streets where 36 kinds of goods were produced for Ly dynasty. In that case, you can consider 2 ways from Noibai Airport to Old Quarter. Taxi or Airport Minibus. Taxi costs around VND360,000 and VND40,000 (equivalent to US$2.00) for Airport Minibus. They take around 40 minutes from airport to Old Quarter.

In case of Airport Minibus, you have to walk around 20 minutes from the final stop of the bus to your lodge at Old Quarter. Therefore, you'd better take a taxi when you arrive at the airport at night rather than Airport Minibus. On the other hand, Airport Minibus is recommended for your way back to the airport.

If you move to other cities of Vietnam from Hanoi, you may use domestic flights. Then, you have to move from Noibai Airport to Terminal 1 which is for domestic departure. A shuttle waiting at the outside of the arrival hall of Noibai Airport, will take you Terminal 1 free.

(Taxi at Noibai Airport)

(Taxi stand is located on the left when you come out of the arrival hall of Noibai Airport.)

(Taxi Stand. They are all meter taxi. Now, you don't need to worry about negotiation on the fare.)

(You are running on the highway by taxi from Noibai Airport to Old Quarter. It takes around 40 minutes and costs about VND360,000, equivalent to US$16.00.)

(Free shuttle at Noibai Airport towards Teminal 1 for domestic flights.)

(Bus stand for free shuttle to Terminal 1 is located on the right side when you come out of the Arrival Hall of Noibai Airport. The bus stand for Airport Minibus is situated on the other side of that for free shuttle.)

(Take this bus for domestic airlines and it will take you to Terminal 1. Airport Minibus is waiting at the other side of the road seen behind the shuttle.)

(An Airport Minibus is waiting for passengers on the other side of the bus stand for the shuttle bus for Terminal 1. The minibus gives shuttle service between Noibai Airport and Vietnam Airline Office near Lake Hoan Kiem. The airline office is located around 1 Km away from Old Quarter where your lodge is situated.)

(Airport Minibus is arriving at the other side of Vietnam Airlines Office near Lake Hoan Kiem. From here, it starts towards Noibai Airport every 1 hour. VND40,000 or US$2.00 for one way.)

(Way from Old Quarter to the bus stand of Airport Minibus.)

Even you use a taxi at Noibai Airport, Airport Minibus is strongly recommended for your return to the airport after finish of your journey at Hanoi. It's quite cheap and good for your experience as a budget traveler. It takes around 20 minutes on foot from Old Quarter to the bus stand for Airport Minibus.

Assuming that you stay at Gia Thinh Hotel located on the road of Hang Bac at Old Quarter, it takes about 20 minutes to the bus stand. Gia Thinh Hotel, cheap and convenient, will be introduced in detail later for budget travelers.

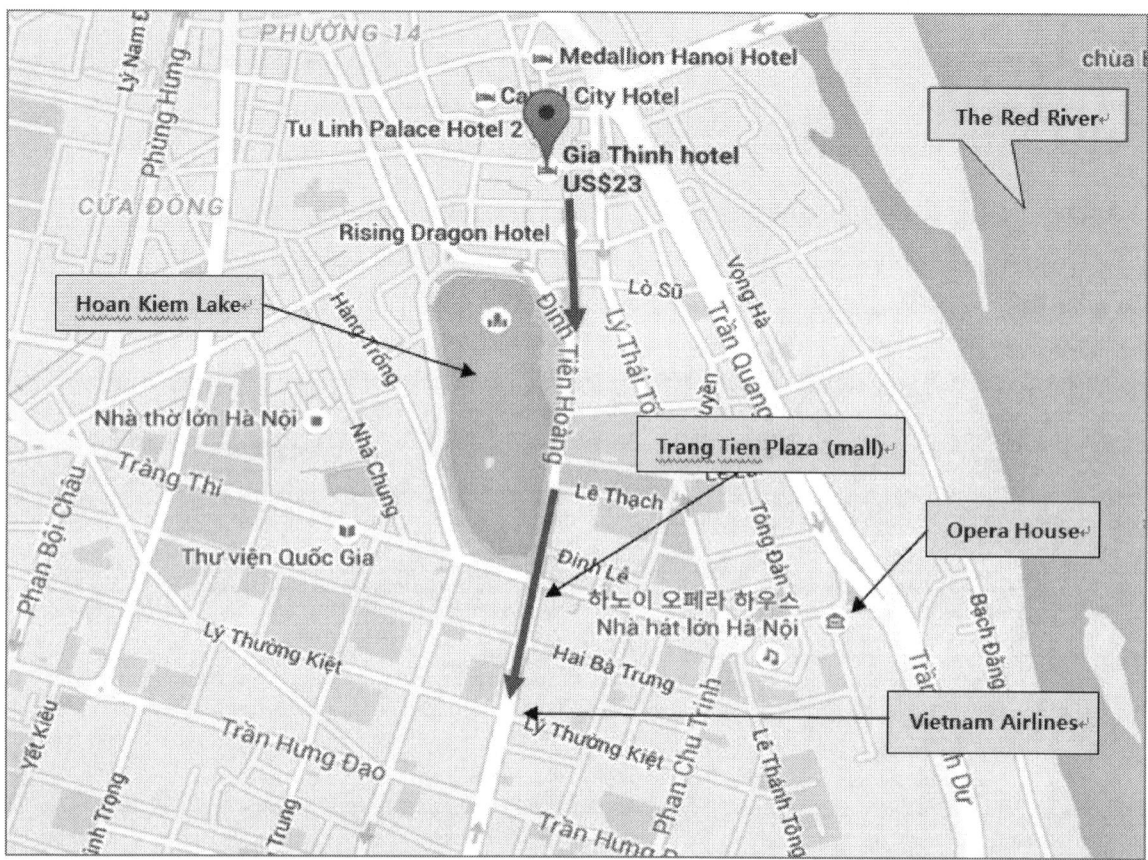

(At first, go to the right when you stand in front of Gia Thin Hotel with you back to the hotel. Then, take the first road on your right. It's Hang Be Road. Go straight Hang Be Street and you will walk on Ding Tien Hoang Road as indicated by the first red arrow on the map.

When you stand at the southern end of Lake Hoan Kiem, you will meet a crossroad with the famous mall of "Trang Tien Plaza" on your left. Go straight 2 blocks more as the second arrow and you will find Vietnam Airlines on your left. The bus stand for Airport Minibus is located on the other side of the airline office.)

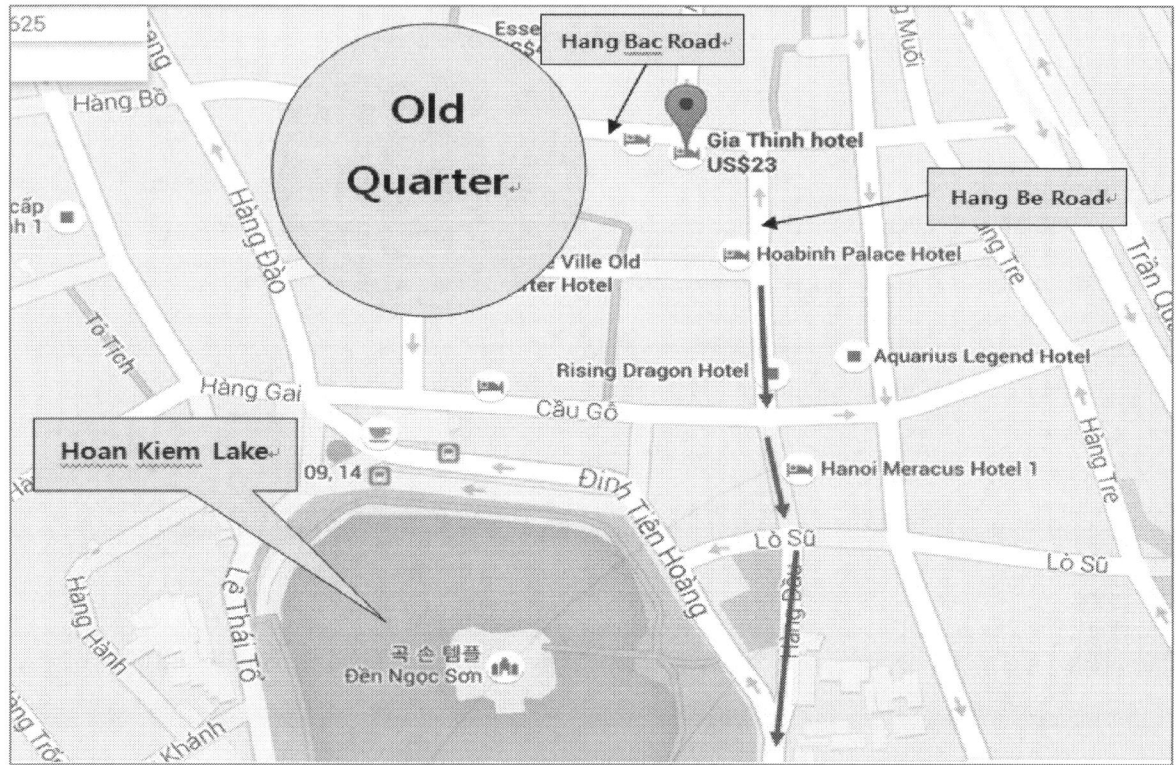

(When you come to the right around 50 meters from Gia Thinh Hotel, you will find a road on your right. It's Hang Be Road. Go straight on the street of Hang Be as the first red arrow on the map. Then, you will come across Dinh Tien Hoang Road by Lake Hoan Kiem.)

(You are standing in front of Gia Thinh Hotel and looking to the right. Go this way around 50 meters and turn to the right. It's Hang Be Road.)

(At the end of Hang Be Road, you are looking at the wide road of Dinh Tien Hoang by Lake Hoan Kiem which is located behind the trees seen on the right. Follow this road against the direction where motorbikes are running to.)

(From the promenade by Lake Hoan Kiem, you are looking at Dinh Tien Hoang Road. At the end of this road, you will meet a crossroad with Trang Tien Plaza on the left. Then, cross the road straight and go 2 blocks more.)

(You are standing at the southern end of Lake Hoan Kiem. The luxurious shopping mall of "Trang Tien Plaza" is standing on the left corner at the crossroad. Cross the road towards Hang Bai Road and go 2 blocks straight more along the road. Then, you will meet Vietnam Airlines on your left.

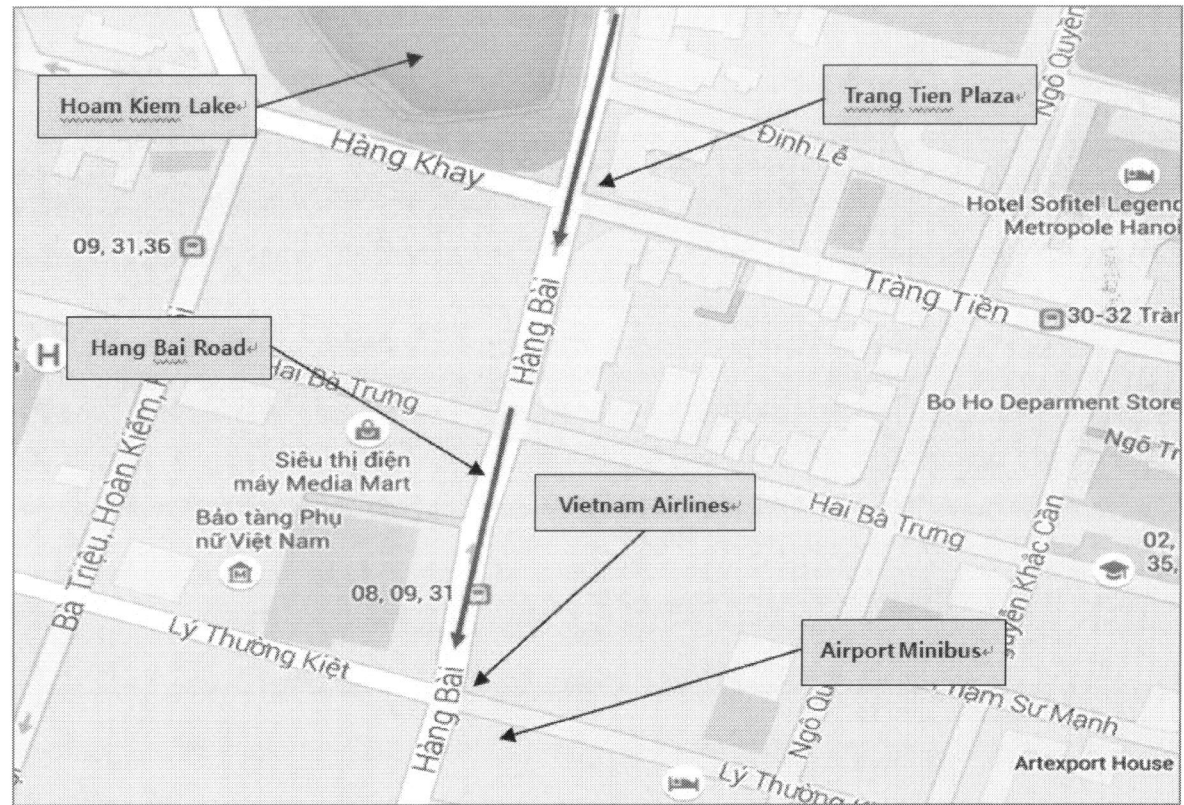

(Airport Minibus is on the other side of Vietnam Airlines standing on Hang Bai Road.)

(After crossing the road, you are walking on Hang Bai Road. "Trang Tien Plaza" is partly seen left.)

(After "Trang Tien Plaza", you will meet another crossroads like this. Follow the car on the photo and you will meet Vietnam Airlines shortly.)

(Vietnam Airlines on Hang Bai Road is seen on the left.)

(From Vietnam Airlines, you are looking at Airport Minibus on the other side of the road.)

(Airport Minibus is waiting for passenger. Except 04:45 am and 7:30 pm, it starts every hour from 06:00 am until 7:00 pm. VND40,000 or US$2.00.)

(From Airport Minibus, you are looking at Vietnam Airlines (left).)

(2) Tour Bus

When you go to Ha Long Bay or Ninh Binh, you'd better use tour bus. It takes around 4 hours to Ha Long Bay and 3 hours for Ninh Binh. They come to your hotel to pickup at 8:30 in the morning and drop you near your hotel when return. A minibus for 20 persons is cool and convenient. Guide speaks English well. Only compare the price between the suggestion by your hotel and that from tourist agencies before booking. Even Ha Long Bay, one day tour would be enough.

(A tour bus is waiting for travelers at Old Quarter before 8:30 in the morning.)

(A tour bus run by a travel agent of "Art Travel".)

3. Hotel

Gorgeous hotels such as Hotel Metropole, Hilton are all located at the street of Trang Tien which can be called as a Luxury Road. On the other hand, cheap and convenient hotels are crowded at Old Quarter, the most beloved hot spot by travelers from all over the world.

Here introduces a hotel named "Gia Thinh Hotel" which is located at the most bustling street of "Hang Bac" at Old Quarter. Hang Bac Road is one of the main streets of Old Quarter which consists of 36 streets. Hang Bac Street has so many hotels, travel agencies, pubs, shops, restaurants, markets, galleries and attractions. You can get Lake Hoan Kiem, one of the must-visits of Hanoi, in 10 minutes on foot. The address of Gia Thinh Hotel is "19 Hang Bac Street, Hoan Kiem District, Old Quarter, Hanoi, Vietnam".

If you take a taxi from Noibai Airport, it costs around VND360,000 and takes approximately 40 minutes to Gia Thinh Hotel at Old Quarter.

(You are walking on the street of "Ma May" at Old Quarter. Gia Thinh Hotel at Hang Bac Road is standing at the end of this road. "Ma May" Road and "Hang Bac Street" is linked each other. On Sundays, they block the entrance to "Ma May Road" for pedestrians and various kinds of performance are held on the street.)

(From the main gate of Gia Thinh Hotel, you are looking at Ma May Road in the morning. Go this Road and you will meet countless shops, pubs, hotels, restaurants and travel agencies.)

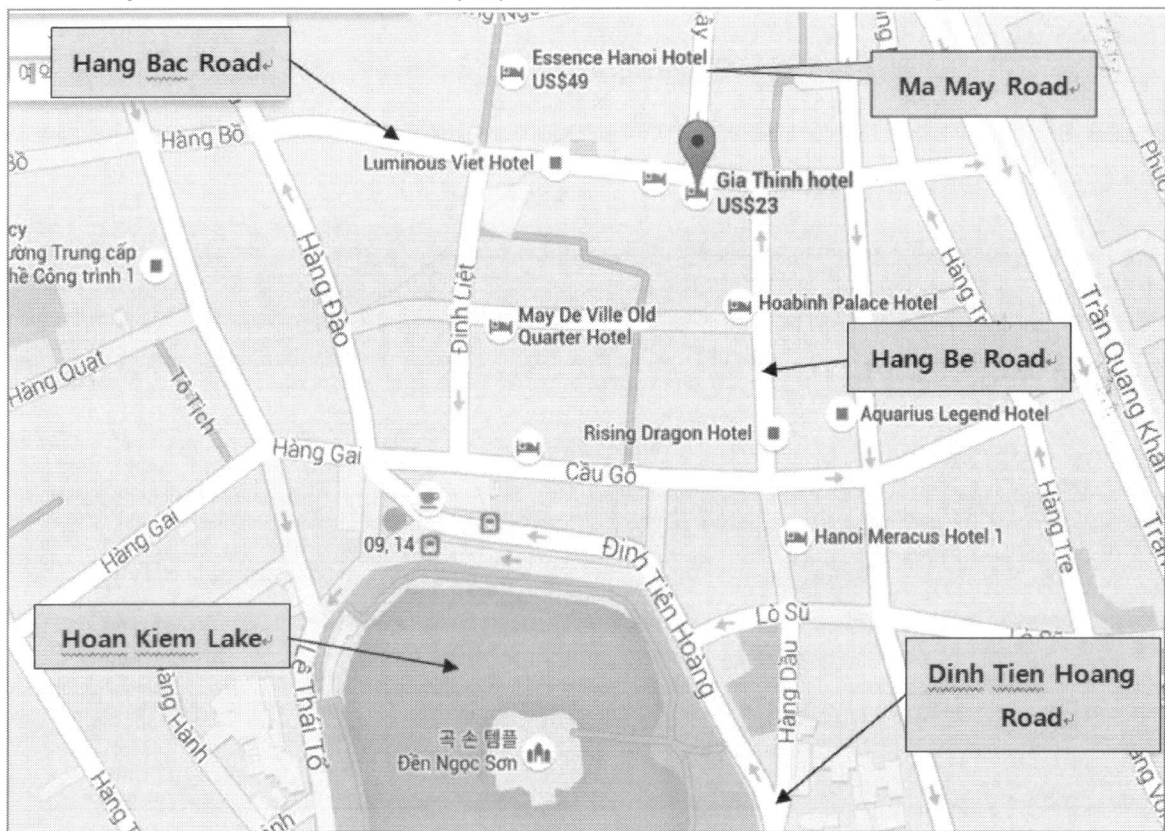

(Ma May Road is sitting just in front of Gia Thinh Hotel. From the hotel, go around 50 meters to the right and you will meet "Hang Be Road". And, walk along the road around 5 minutes and you will meet Hoan Kiem Lake.)

(Front Desk. Restaurant for your breakfast is partly seen on the right. You can ask them for your one day tour to Ha Long Bay or Ninh Binh. Compare the price with those of travel agencies before booking.)

(Restaurant. Small but clean and delicious. Choose dishes you want first and baguette, butter, jam, egg fries with bacon and fruits will be servied.)

4. Attractions

Travel to Hanoi can be largely divided into 2 parts. One is Hanoi itself and the other is outskirts such as Ha Long Bay and Ninh Binh. Hanoi also can be divided into 2 parts. One is the bustling downtown such as Old Quarter and Lake Hoan Kiem. The other is Ho Chi Minh's Mausoleum Complex.

Here introduces Old Quarter and Hoan Kiem Lake first. And, Ha Long Bay and Ninh Binh will be followed.

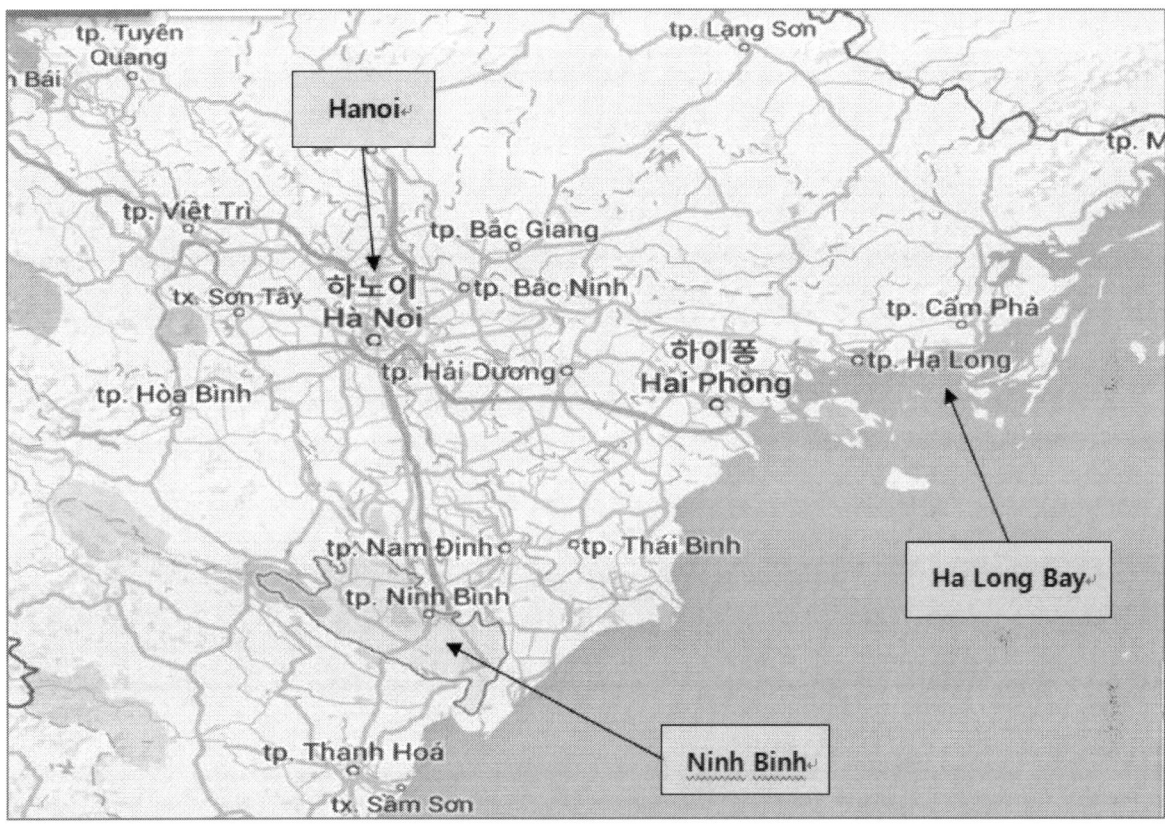

(It takes around 4 hours by tour bus from Hanoi to Ha Long Bay and 3 hours to Ninh Binh.)

(Map for the attractions at Old Quarter and Lake Hoan Kiem.)

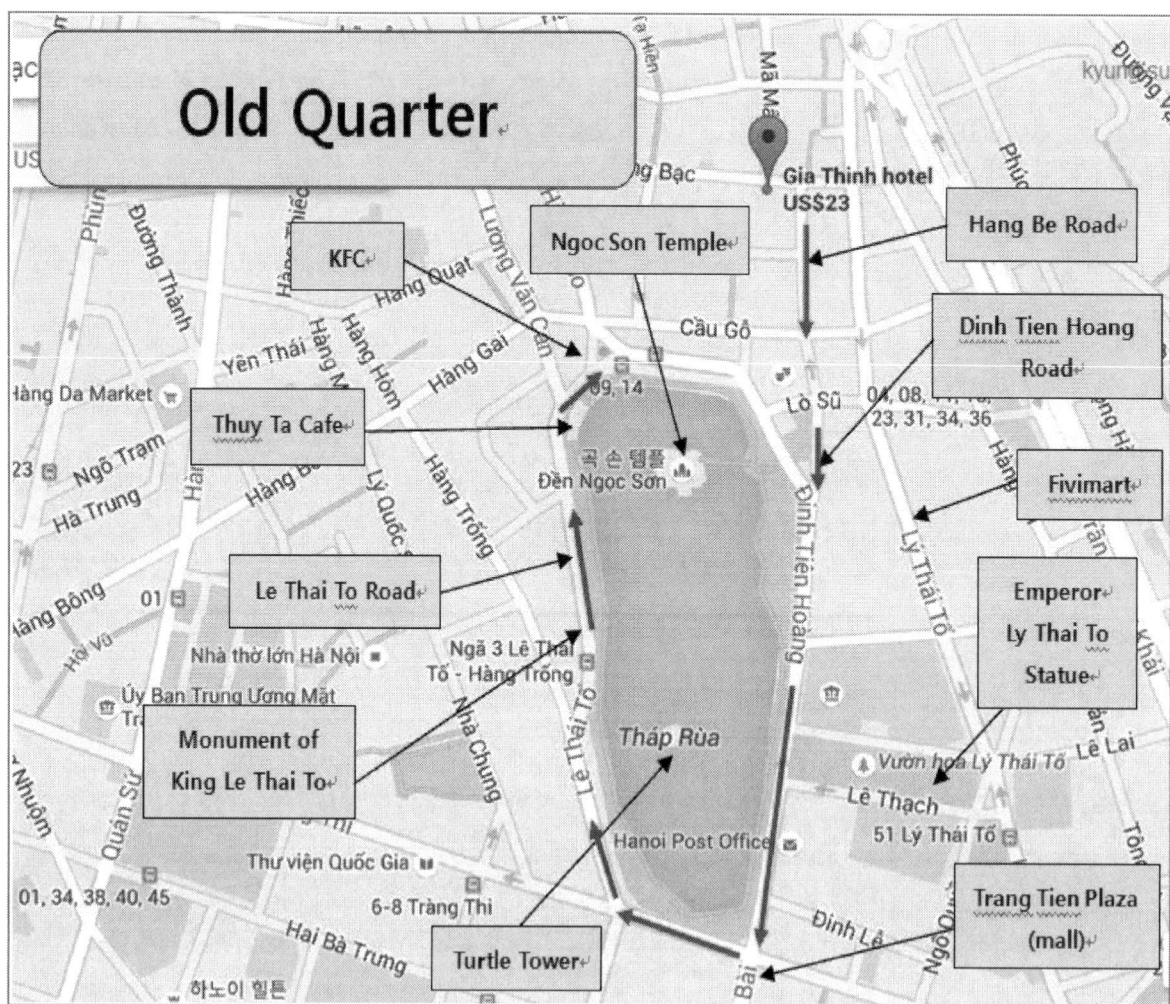

(Old Quarter, in other words "36 Streets", which is located at the northern part of Lake Hoan Kiem, is introduced first and attractions around the lake will be followed. You can call Old Quarter as a travelers' street.

This book tells you the way to the attractions in assumption that your lodge is situate at Old Quarter like Gia Thinh Hotel which has been introduced earlier.

Therefore, if you take the road of "Hang Be" indicated by a box on the upper right side of the map, you will automatically meet the Lake Hoan Kiem in 10 minutes. As shown on the map, if you take a stroll around the lake, you can pay visits the whole attractions at Hoan Kiem Lake.

Now, let's go to Old Quarter first.

(1) Old Quarter ("36 Streets")

Old Quarter can be called the heart of Hanoi. Emperor Ly Thai To who moved the capital city from Hoa Lu to "Thang Long (currently Hanoi)" in 1010, gathered craftsmen all over the country for the goods to be used by government. And, the craftsmen settled near royal palace and formed 36 streets by goods they produced. For example, Hang Bac Street was the road for silver and Hang Da Street was for leather. Hang Muoi Road was for salt and Hang Ma Street for paper and so forth. "Hang" means "goods".

They call the district of 36 streets as Old Quarter. Even now, there are many silver shops at Hang Bac Road where Gia Thinh Hotel is sitting. Old Quarter has so many shops, hotels, restaurants, pubs, travel agencies and markets. You may be confused at the bustling streets crowded with tour buses to pickup travelers, motorbikes to workplace and cyclos even early in the morning.

At night, you might not pass the roads without sitting on a chair like local people with a cup of "Bia Hoi" on the road. "Bia Hoi" is the Vietnamese traditional draft beer with 2 alcoholic degree. They produce Bia Hoi every early in the morning and deliver it to the shops. They drink it like a tea. Bia Hoi is cheap and fresh. It costs only VND5,000 a cup of Bia Hoi.

One more thing you have not to pass over, is kebob. They put so many kinds of meat and vegetable in a big piece of baguette to make a kebob. With a cup of Bia Hoi and a kebob, you can make a good dinner on the road. Kebob is cheap, tasty and enough for a meal.

(Travelers are enjoying Bia Hoi and kebob on the road of Old Quarter.)

(Map for the streets at Old Quarter)

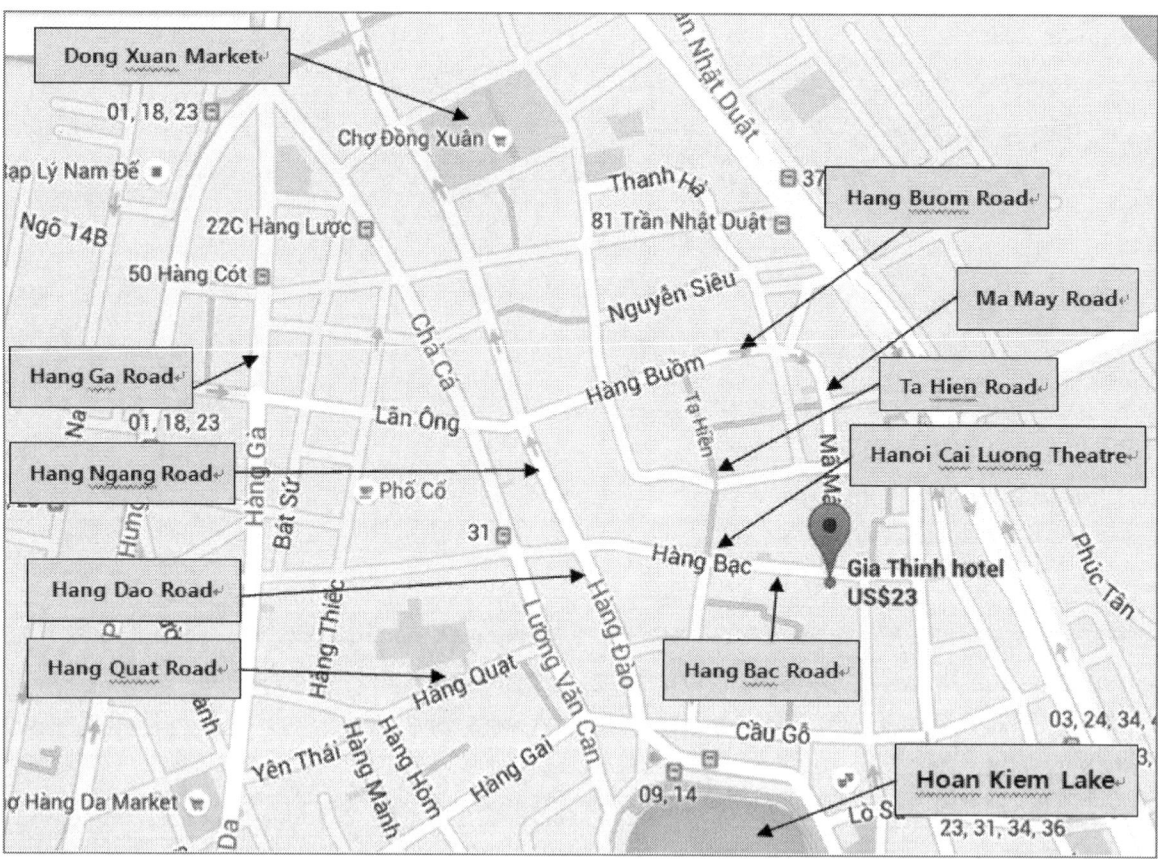

(Old Quarter (36 Streets) is located on the northern district of Hoan Kiem Lake.

Gia Thinh Hotel is situated at Hang Bac Road of Old Quarter. When you stand at the road with your back to Gia Thinh Hotel, you will automatically meet Ma May Road sitting in front of you. The easiest way to look at one of the real faces of Old Quarter, take a stroll along Ma May Road.

From the hotel at Hang Bac Road, go 1 block to the left and you will meet "Hanoi Cai Luong Theatre" on your right. If you go one more block from the theater, you will stand at a crossroads. Take the street of Hang Ngang at the crossroads and you will meet "Dong Xuan Market" in around 5 minutes.

If you pay a visit "Jewelry Communal House" located between Gia Thinh Hotel and "Hanoi Cai Luang Theater", you will come to know the history of Hang Bac Road. "Hang Quat Road" shown on the lower left has many silk shops.

Now, let's go to "Ma May Road" first for you journey to Old Quarter.)

(Ma May Street)

(You are standing in front of Gia Thinh Hotel at Hang Bac Road and looking at Ma May Road where minibuses are waiting travelers. Motorbikes are running on Hang Bac Road.)

(Ma May Street. Countless pubs and shops, hotels and restaurants are crowded at this road. At night rather than daytime, Ma May Road is bustling with travelers and local people.)

(Pub "Newday". Situated "72 Ma May" as shown on its signboard.)

(Ma May Street is blocked on Sundays for pedestrians. No cars on Sundays and various kinds of performance are held on the street.)

(On a Sunday, a Vietnamese traditional performance is held on Ma May Road.)

(A famous street bar with kebob. Travelers are enjoying "Bia Hoi", the traditional Vietnamese beer, on the street of Ma May. Your try a cup of "Bia Hoi" together with a kebob is strongly recommended. Kebob will be prepared on demand.)

(The owner of the beer pub is preparing a kebob. He pours meat and vegetable into the baguette. It's really delicious and full enough for a meal. VND30,000.)

(Cafe heaven at "Ta Hien Road" which is automatically linked with "Ma May Street".)

(Cafe heaven overcrowded with travelers and local people.)

(All sit on the street with a cup of "Bia Hoi".)

(Travelers are checking menu at a restaurant on Ma May Road.)

(Bike Rental)

(Another cart bar on the street. She sells grilled chicken skewer and kebob.)

(So many pubs on the street.)

(Shops on both sides are selling "Bia Hoi" and kebob. The name of the shop seen in front is "Thang Hang". VND5,000 for a cup of "Bia Hoi" and VND30,000 for a kebob.)

(Take a chair prepared on the road and he or she will come to you for taking order.)

(Sinh Tourist (blue signboard) at Ma May Road. Sinh Tourist is one of the most famous travel agencies in Vietnam. Except Sinh Tourist, there are many kinds of travel agencies at the street.)

(You are walking on the street of Ma May to return to Gia Thinh Hotel standing at Hang Bac Road. Hang Bac Road and Ma May Street are linked each other.)

(Jewelry Communal House & Dong Xuan Market at Hang Bac Road.)

(At Gia Thinh Hotel on Hang Bac Road, you are looking right early in the morning.)

(You are looking left at Gia Thih Hotel standing on Hang Bac Road. Go around 50 meters and you will meet Jewelry Communal House on your right. If you walk one block from here, you will also meet Hanoi Cai Luong Theater on the right. Jewelry Communal House is located between Gia Thinh Hotel and Hanoi Cai Luong Theater.)

(Jewelry Communal House. You can learn about the history of Hang Bac Street here.)

(Jewelry Communal House)

(You are looking back at "Hanoi Cai Luong Theatre" seen on the left corner of the crossroads. Follow the red arrow on the photo and go one more block. Then, you will meet another crossroads. Take the street of "Hang Ngang" for "Dong Xuan Market" at the junction.)

(Follow the cyclo or the green taxi and you will meet "Dong Xuan Market" on the right in 10 minutes. The street to the market is "Hang Ngang Road". Signs standing at this crossroads will confirm you.)

(Dong Xuan Market (left). Silk goods and accessories. Motorbikes are running on Hang Gnang Road.)

(Inside "Dong Xuan Market".)

(Hang Be Road and other faces of Old Quarter.)

(Hang Be Road. From Gia Thinh Hotel at Hang Bac Road, go around 50 meters to the right. Then, you will find this road on your right. If you follow this road, you will meet Lake Hoan Kiem in 5 minutes. A gallery is situated on the corner and a small market will be held on the right side of the photo.)

(A fruit shop at the market. Fresh and cheap. This shop is located just by the gallery.)

(A raw meat shop on the opposite side of the gallery.)

(Another market at Old Quarter.)

(You will meet various kinds of fruit at every market.)

(They sell raw meat and traditional rice noodle on the road.)

(Baguette and grilled skewer.)

(Fruits on the street.)

(You will meet so many street cafe for a meal.)

(2) Hoan Kiem Lake

Lake Hoan Kiem at southern Old Quarter is around 700 meters long and 400 meters wide. When you walk along the road of Hang Be from Gia Thinh Hotel standing at Hang Bac Street of Old Quarter, you will meet Hoan Kiem Lake in 10 minutes. And, Ngoc Son Pagoda at the lake would be seen first.

If you remember the 2 streets of "Dinh Tien Hoang" and "Le Thai To", it would be much helpful for you to find attractions around the lake. "Dinh Tien Hong Road" is running on the right side of the lake and "Le Thai To Street" goes on the other side of the lake.

When you take a stroll along the promenade well-prepared around Hoan Kiem Lake, you will meet "Emperor Ly Thai To Statue" first which is standing on the wide street of "Dinh Tien Hoang". "Dinh Tien Hoang" is a king of old Vietnam who took "Hoa Lu" as its capital.

At the southern part of the lake, you will find the "Turtle Tower" which is standing in the lake. The legend of the lake says that general "Le Loi (1385~1433)" received a divine sword from a turtle of the lake and succeeded independence from China. After victory, he returned the sword to the turtle as promised and he took the crown as "King Le Thai To", not "Emperor Ly Thai To". They are different.

Turn to the right from the end of the lake, you will meet "Monument of King Le Thai To" shortly. And, the beautiful restaurant of "Thuy Ta Cafe" is waiting for you at the upper end of the lake. Another cafe "Garden" beautifully covered with flowers sits just by the restaurant.

When you come out of "Thuy Ta Cafe" after a rest, you will find a fountain standing in the middle of a vast rotary. A KFC is on the left side of the fountain and a 5 storied building which is packed with so many restaurants and cafes such as Highlands Coffee and Lake View Cafe, is standing on the opposite side of the rotary. Behind the tall building of cafes, Old Quarter begins.

It's the end of the round trip to Lake Hoan Kiem.

Therefore, this book goes (1) Ngoc Son Pagoda first along the street of "Dinh Tien Hoang". And, (2) Statue of Emperor Ly Thai To, (3) Turtle Tower, (4) "Monument of King Le Thay To" on the road of "Le Thai To", (5) Thuy Ta Cafe and (6) Fivimart (Aeon) on "Ly Thai To Road" will be followed.

(From the promenade well-prepared by the street of "Dinh Tien Hoang", you are looking back at the pedestrian road by Lake Hoan Kiem. The legendary "Turtle Tower" is standing far left on the lake. If you go straight this way to the end, you will meet Old Quarter.)

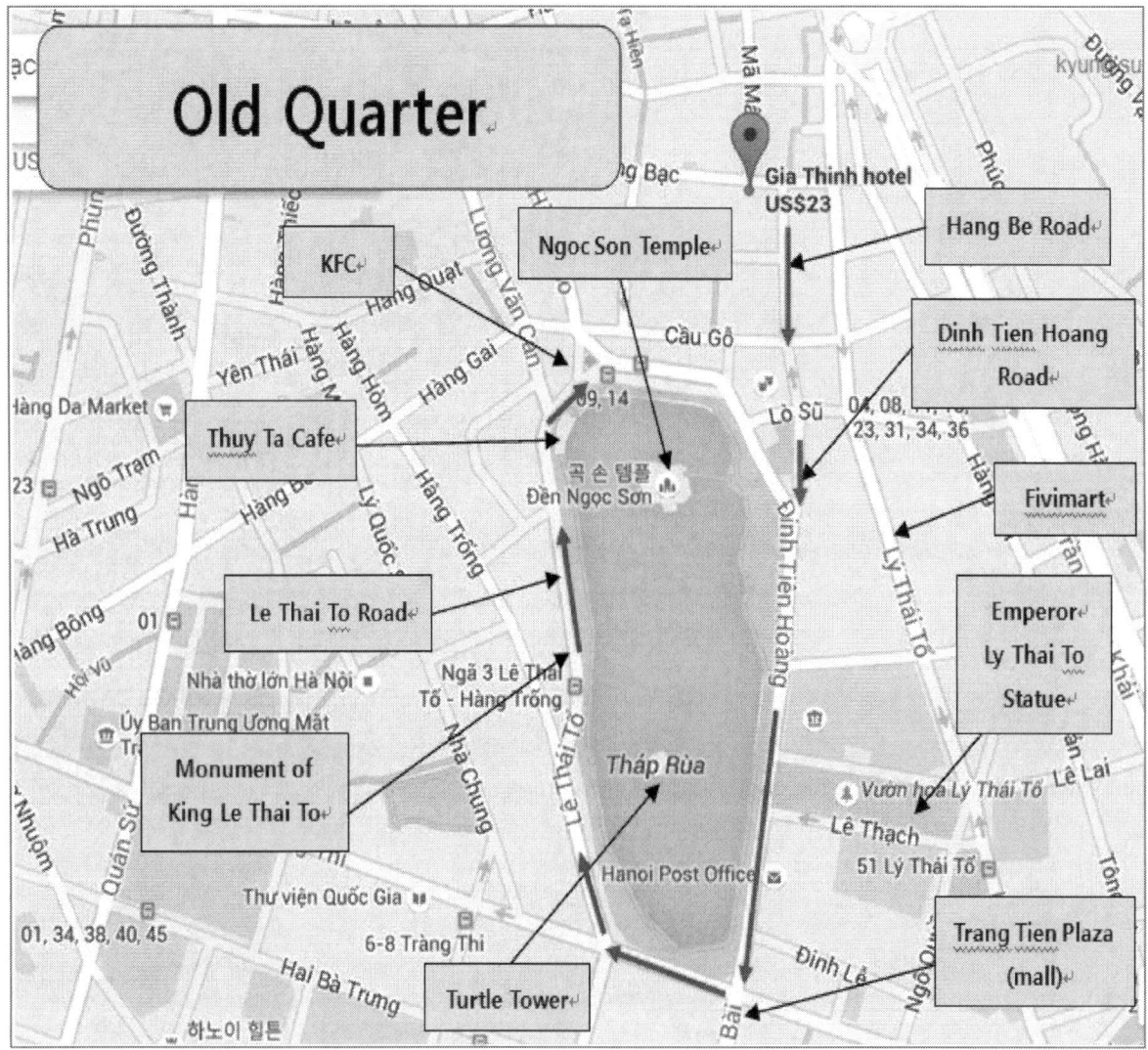

(Your trip to Lake Hoan Kime will follow the red arrows starting from "Hang Be Road" of Old Quarter. When you come to the right around 50 meters from Gia Thinh Hotel at Hang Bac Road, you will meet "Hang Be Road" shortly on your right. Go along Hang Be Road and you will automatically meet the wide street of "Dinh Tien Hoang" by Lake Hoan Kiem.

After "Emperor Ly Thai To Statue", you will meet a luxurious shopping mall of "Trang Tien Plaza" which is standing on a corner at a wide crossroads. If you follow the street of "Trang Tien" lying by the mall of "Trang Tien Plaza", you will find "Opera House" at the end of the road. There are gorgeous hotels such as Hilton and Metropole together with the luxurious mall of Prada are all located around Opera House.

Turn to the right at the southern end of the lake, you will meet "Monument of King Le Thai To" shortly which is standing on the street of "Le Thia To" running on the left side of the lake. Free entrance to the monument but no short sleeves, no short pants nor slippers into the shrine behind the monument.

After "Monument of King Le Thai To", you will meet the beautiful restaurant of "Thuy Ta Cafe" at the upper end of the lake. "Garden", another small cafe by the restaurant, is covered with beautiful flowers.

Come out of the restaurant of "Thuy Ta Cafe" and you will find a vast rotary with a fountain. A KFC is on the left side from the fountain and a 5-story-building packed with cafes and restaurants is standing on the opposite side of the rotary.

Fivimart (Aeon) will be introduced at the finish. It is a huge supermarket situated at the street of "Ly Thai To" which is one block away from "Dinh Tien Hoang Road" by Hoan Kiem Lake. Considering not so many big supermarkets at Old Quarter, Fivimart would be much helpful for travelers. Fivimart is located not far from Emperor Ly Thai To Statue.

(2-1) Ngoc Son Pagoda

"Ngoc Son Pagoda" was built on the lake in 1864. "Ngoc Son", "玉山" in Chinese, means "Jade Mountain" looking like a small mountain on the green lake. They enshrined General "Tran Hung Dao" who defeated Mongolian invasion in the 13th century and Guan Yu, a famous Chinese hero and other heroes at Ngoc Son Pagoda. VND30,000.

(Way to Ngoc Son Pagoda)

(Way from Old Quarter to Ngoc Son Pagoda)

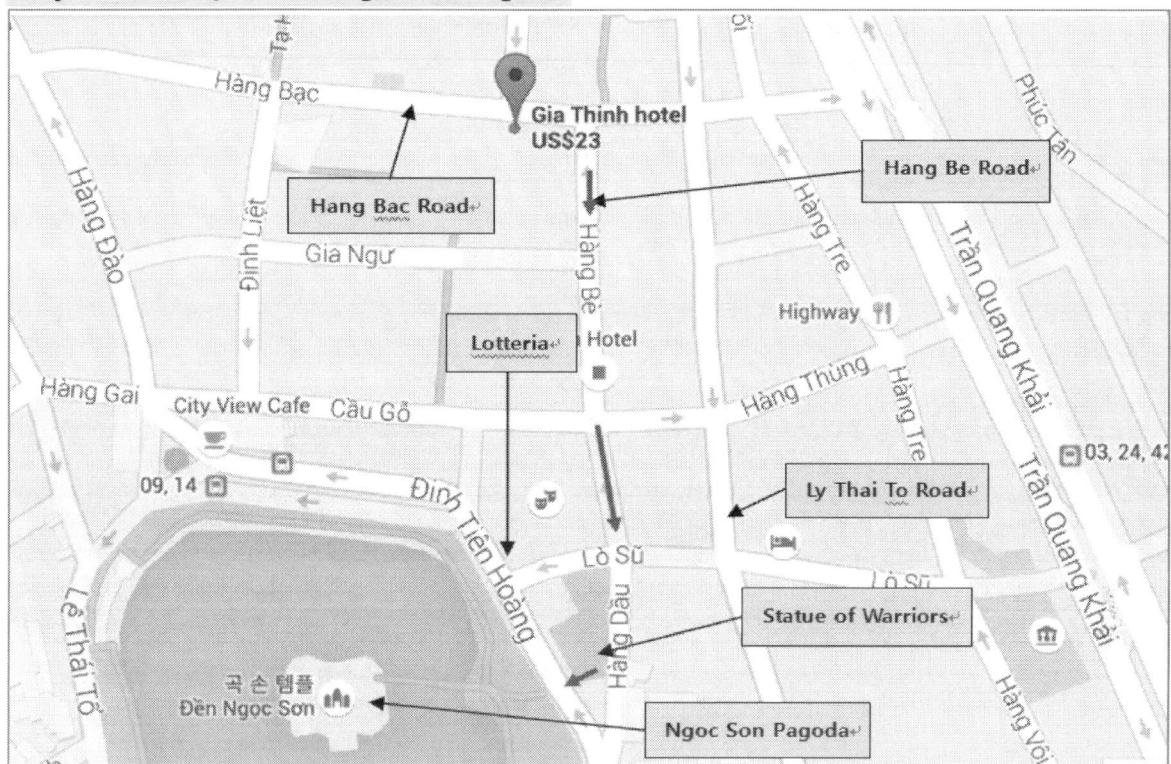

(Go right 50 meters from Gia Thinh Hotel standing on Hang Bac Road and you will meet "Hang Be Road" on your right. Follow straight along the road as indicated by the red arrows on the map and you will stand at "Statue of Warriors" in 10 minutes. There you can see the entrance to Ngoc Son Pagoda on the other side of the road, "Dinh Tien Hoang".)

(At Gia Thinh Hotel, you are looking right. Motorbikes are running on Hang Bac Road. Go around 50 meters along this road and you will meet the street of "Hang Be" on your right.)

(Hang Be Road. Go straight and you will meet "Statue of Warriors" shortly.)

("Statue of Warriors". "Ngoc Son Pagoda" is standing on the other side of the road.)

(Entrance to "Ngoc Son Pagoda". Cross the road of "Dinh Tien Hoang" seen on the photo.)

(The gate to Ngoc Son Pagoda is protected by a tiger on the left and a dragon on the right. They call them "Tiger Door (虎 門)" and "Dragon Door (龍 門).)

(A tall pagoda is standing at the entrance.)

(Way to "Ngoc Son Pagoda".)

(You are looking at "Ngoc Son Pagoda" from the park by Lake Hoan Kiem. The red bridge partly seen on the far right will take you to "Ngoc Son Pagoda".)

(Cross the red bridge and you will meet "Ngoc Son Pagoda". Ticket box is hidden on the left.)

(Ticket box. Buy a ticket and you can cross the bridge to Ngoc Son Pagoda. VND30,000 (children under 15 is VND15,000).)

("Hoan Kiem Lake")

(From the entrance to "Ngoc Son Pagoda", you are looking at the picturesque promenade along the lake of Hoan Kiem.)

(Park by the Lake Hoan Kiem.)

(You are looking back at "Ngoc Son Pagoda" (red flags).)

(The legendary "Turtle Tower" is standing far on the Lake Hoan Kiem.)

(There are many giant trees and beautiful flowers in the park. The road on the right is "Dinh Tien Hoang Street".)

(A long pedestrian road is prepared by the park. Motorbikes are running on the street of "Dinh Tien Hoang" seen on the left.)

(2-2) Statue of Emperor Ly Thai To

When you follow "Dinh Tien Hoang Street", you will find "Emperor Ly Thai To Statue" standing on the other side of the road. He established Ly Dynasty and moved the capital city from "Hoa Lu" to "Thang Long", currently "Hanoi", in 1010. He named the new capital "Thang Long (昇 龍)" which means "Ascending Dragon" after he saw a dragon flying from the Red River to the sky. The Red River is not far from Lake Hoan Kiem.

Emperor Ly Thai To is different from "King Le Thai To" who lived between 1385 and 1433 who made Vietnamese independence from China in the 15th century.

They call the road behind the statue as "Ly Thai To". On the other hand, they named the road by the other side of Lake Hoan Kime as "Le Thai To". "Monument of King Le Thai To" is standing on the street of "Le Thai To" which will be introduced later.

(Behind the motorbikes running on the street of "Dinh Tien Hoang", Emperor Ly Thai To Statue is standing in a park.)

(Emperor Ly Thai To. Ruled between 1009 ~ 1029. Another beautiful park is behind the statue.)

(A park behind the statue.)

(From the entrance to "Emperor Ly Thai To Statue", you are looking at "Dinh Tien Hong Road".)

(2-3) Turtle Tower

"Turtle Tower" standing on the lake has a legend. It goes that when General Le Loi (1388~1433) walked by the Lake Hoan Kiem, who was "King Le Thai To" later, a turtle came up from the lake and gave him a divine sword. After achieving independence from China, he returned the sacred sword to the turtle as promised. "Hoan Kiem" is "還 劍" in Chinese. It means "Returning the Sword".

("Turtle Tower")

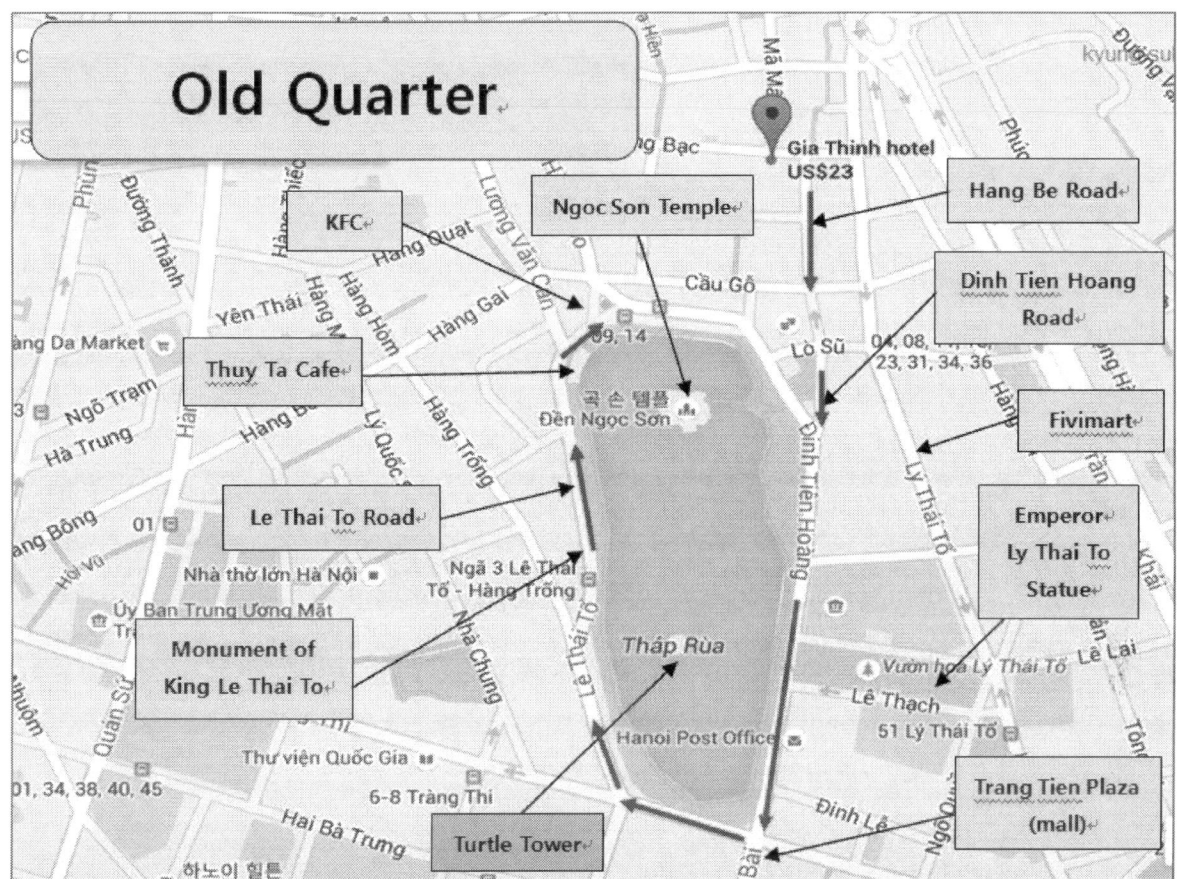

("Turtle Tower" is standing on the southern part of Lake Hoan Kiem. When you pass by "Emperor Ly Thai To Statue", you will meet a small gate standing on the pedestrian road by the lake. It is "報 恩 門", "Gate of Thanks Returning".)

(After Emperor Ly Thai To Statue, you are now taking a stroll on the promenade by the lake. The gate of "報恩門 (Gate of Thanks Returning)" is partly seen on the far left.)

("報 恩 門" means "Gate of Thanks Returning.)

("Hanoi Post Office" (left) is standing by Emperor Ly Thai To Statue on "Dinh Tien Hoang Road".)

(You are looking back at the lake. "Turtle Tower" is seen far left on the lake.)

(After "Hanoi Post Office", you will meet a wide crossroads. A luxurious shopping mall of "Trang Tien Plaza" is standing on a corner of the junction at the southern end of the lake.)

(The southern end of Lake Hoan Kiem.)

(From the southern end of Hoan Kiem Lake, you are looking at "Turtle Tower".)

(2-4) Monument of King Le Thai To

"Monument of King Le Thai To" is a shrine dedicated to King Le Thai To, the main actor of the legend of Lake Hoan Kiem. He was actually a general named "Le Loi" who lived between 1385 and 1433. After independence from China, he wore a crown as King Le Thai To. Free admission but no entrance to the shrine behind the monument with short sleeves, short pants or slippers.

("Monument of King Le Thai To" is standing by the street of "Le Thai To".)

(Monument of King Le Thai To. Free admission.)

("Built in 1896, this monument is closely connected with the legend of retrieving the magic sword on Lake Hoan Kiem.")

(Monument of King Le Thai To)

(An altar behind the monument. The shrine for praying is partly seen behind the altar.)

(You are looking back at the monument.)

(2-5) Thuy Ta Cafe

After "Monument of King Le Thai To", you will meet a beautiful restaurant of "Thuy Ta Cafe" shortly. It is situated just by the upper side of the lake. Another gorgeous cafe, "Garden", covered with beautiful flowers is sitting by "Thuy Ta Cafe".

When you come out of the restaurant after a short break, you will find a vast rotary with a fountain in the middle. A KFC is on the left and a 5-story-building is standing on the right. There are restaurants and cafes such as Highlands Coffee and City View Cafe in the building.

("Thuy Ta Cafe")

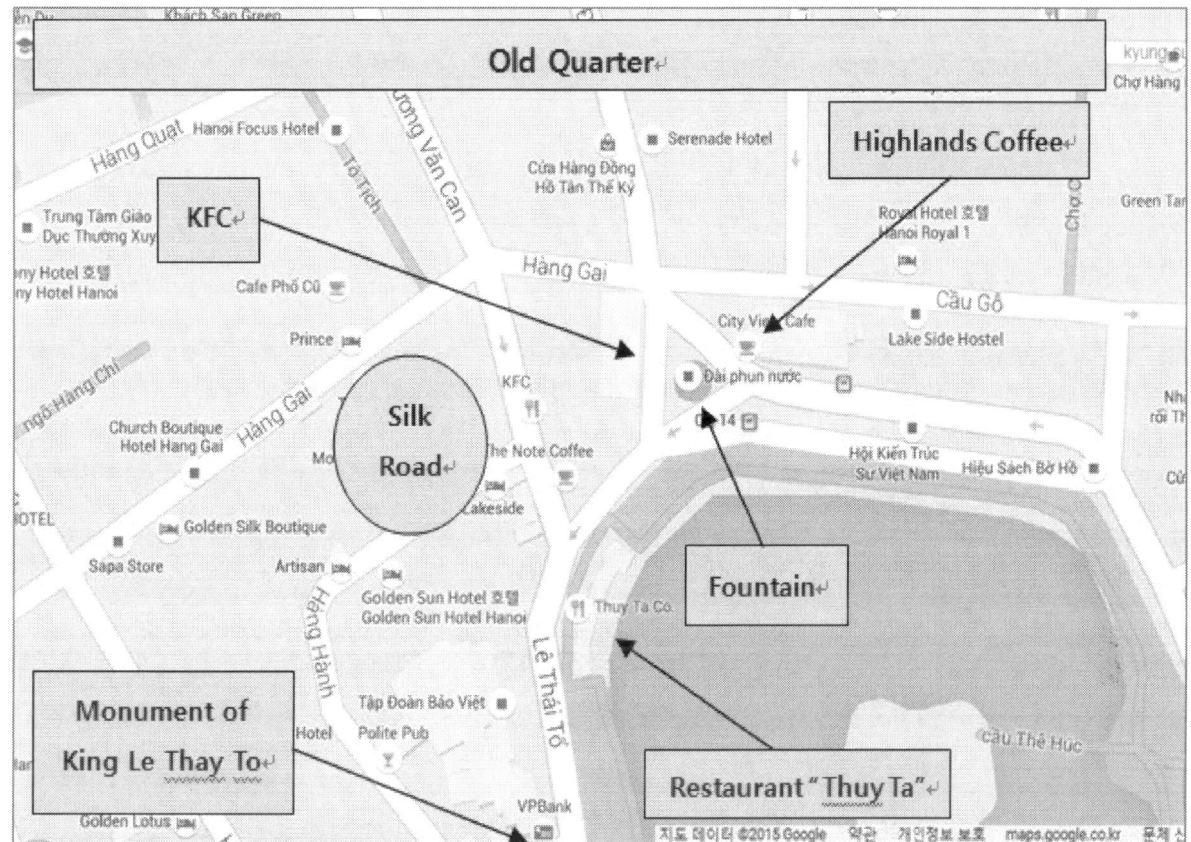

("Thuy Ta Cafe" is sitting just by the lake.)

(You are looking back at "Monument of King Le Thai To" on the way to "Thuy Ta Cafe".)

(Thuy Ta Cafe)

(Very clean and cool.)

(English menu with photos.)

(Roasted dumplings)

(Rice & pork with sauce.)

(Tables prepared outside the restaurant.)

(Thuy Ta Cafe)

(호수 가의 Thuy Ta Cafe 를 돌아보다.)

("Thuy Ta Cafe" casts its feature on the lake.)

(Another cafe "Garden" by the restaurant of "Thay Ta Cafe".)

(You are looking back at "Garden" covered with beautiful flower.)

(You are looking at the rotary from cafe "Garden".)

(A KFC and HSBC are located at the building beside the fountain.)

(From KFC, you are looking at the 5-story-building. It has many restaurants and cafes such as Highlands Coffee, City View Cafe. Malls like "ALDO" and "SWAROVSKI" are situated on the ground floor. It has Legend Beer and Hanoi Korean restaurant, too.)

(2-6) Fivi Mart (Aeon)

It's rare to meet a big supermarket for travelers at Old Quarter. However, you can find a super market situated on the street of "Ly Thai To" near Old Quarter. It's "Fivimart" run by AEON, one of the biggest superstore chains in the world. Nearly almost of all you need can be found at Fivimart.

("Fivimart" on the street of "Ly Thai To".)

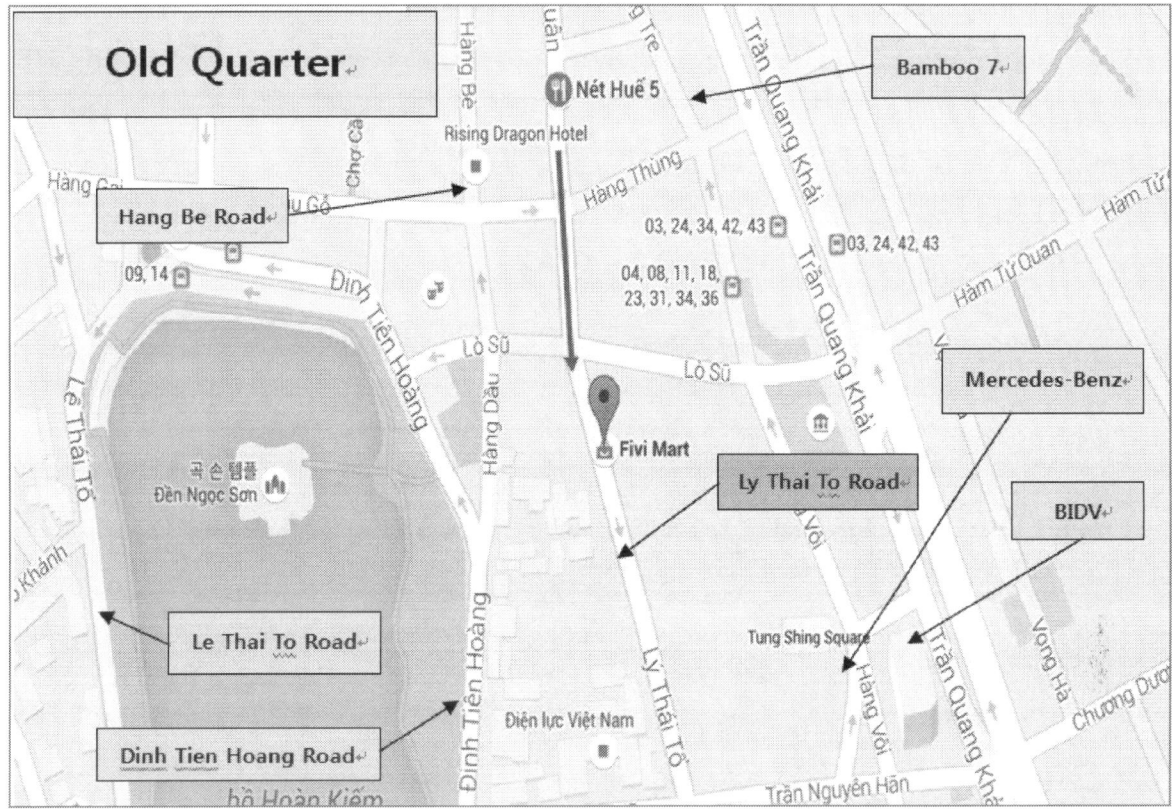

(Take the street next to "Hang Be Road" and you will meet "Fivimart" on "Ly Thai To Road" in 5 minutes.)

(Entrance to Fivimart on the ground floor.)

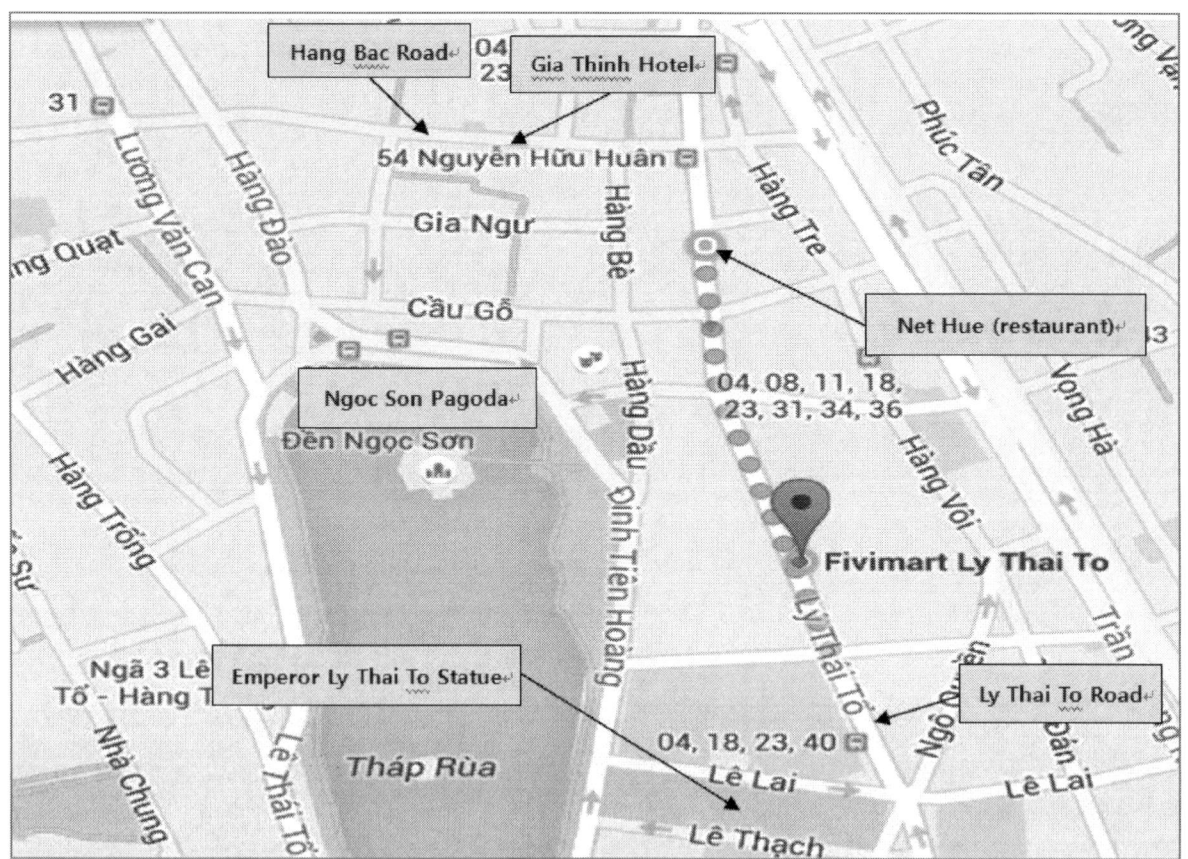

(Fivimart (Aeon) is located around 200 meters from restaurant "Net Hue" which is situated on the next road to "Hang Be Street". From Gia Thinh Hotel on the road of "Hang Bac", go 2 blocks to the right and you will meet "Net Hue" which is situated 50 meters away on the next street to "Hang Be Road", the first road from the hotel.)

(Restaurant "Net Hue". Special for Vietnamese foods. Follow the car parking in front of Net Hue.)

(Net Hue. Beef rolls and rice noodle with vegetable. Put items in the rice paper and try.)

(Cafe "Smile" on the way to "Fivimart".)

(Fivimart)

(Cold storage)

(Fruits and vegetables)

(3) Trang Tien Road

Different from Old Quarter where cheap hotels, pubs, cafes, travel agencies, markets, theaters and shrines are condensed, the street of "Trang Tien" is worth to be called as a "Luxurious Road". "Trang Tien Road" starts from the gorgeous shopping mall of "Trang Tien Plaza" which is situated on the wide crossroads at the southern end of Lake Hoan Kiem.

When you walk along "Trang Tien Street" from "Trang Tien Plaza", you will meet a photo gallery first which displays war-related photos. You can enter the gallery free. Hotel Metropole Hanoi is located behind Citibank's international business center on the road. "Opera House" and Hilton Hotel are sitting at a wide rotary at the end of the road. There you will find Hanoi Stock Exchange and the luxurious shopping mall of "Prada" near Opera House. If you take a walk on the street of "Ly Thai To" lying by "Prada", you will meet Casa Italia and National Bank of Vietnam.

(Opera House. Hilton Hotel is standing on the right.)

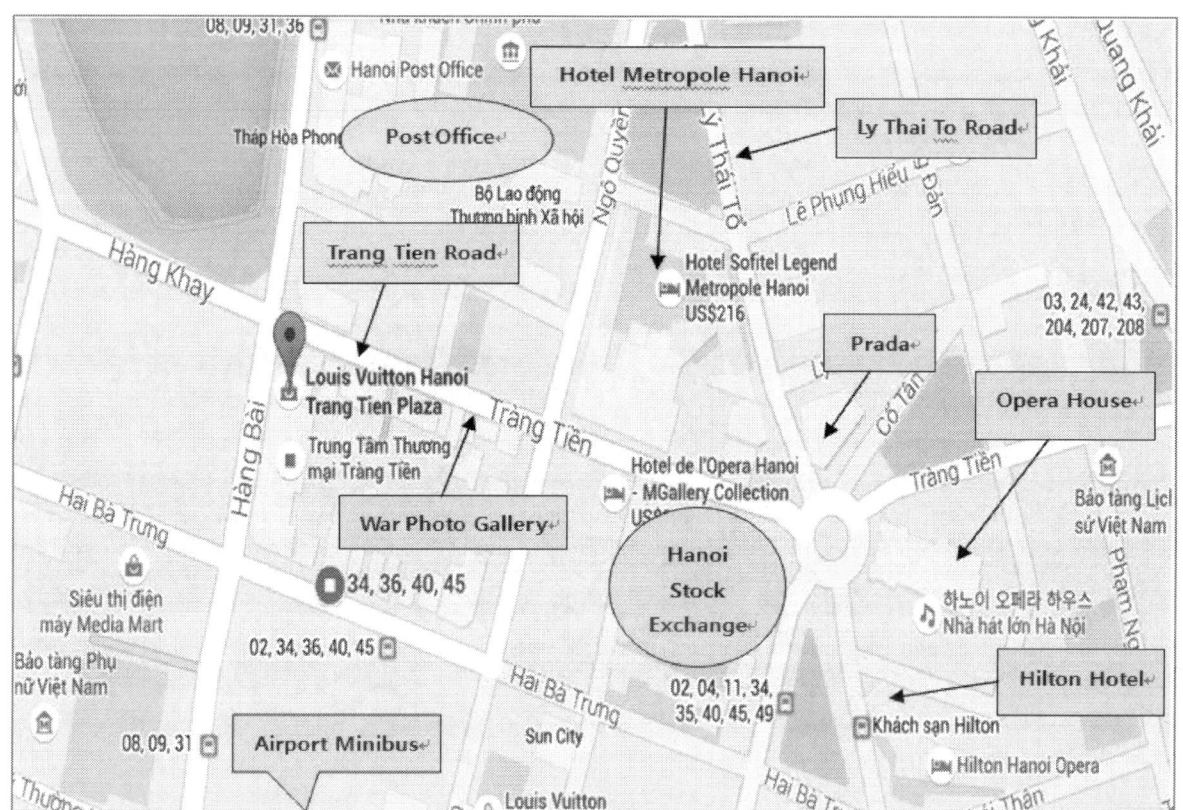

("Trang Tien Road" starts from the shopping mall of "Trang Tien Plaza" which is standing at the end of Lake Hoan Kiem. A red mark on the map indicates the mall. After war photo gallery, you will meet Citibank on a corner shortly. Hotel Metropole Hanoi is situated behind the bank.

When you stand at Hanoi Stock Exchange, you will easily find Opera House and Hilton Hotel on the opposite side of a wide rotary. Another luxurious shopping mall of "Prada" is also standing on the left. The street of "Ly Thai To" is lying by the mall. If you pass by Casa Italia and National Bank of Vietnam located on the street, you will finally meet "Fivimart(AEON)" on the same road of "Ly Thai To".)

(You are looking at "Trang Tien Plaza" standing on a corner at the southern end of Lake Hoan Kiem. Motorbikes and cars are rushing out of the street of "Trang Tien". You will meet "Opera House" at the end of the road.)

(Trang Tien Plaza)

(Trang Tien Plaza at night.)

(Dior at Trang Tien Plaza)

(You are looking back at "Trang Tien Plaza". A bookstore is next to the mall.)

(An Arts Gallery at Trang Tien Road.)

(Vietnam : The Real War : A photographic History by Associated Press.)

101

(A photo exhibited at the war history gallery. The last helicopter.)

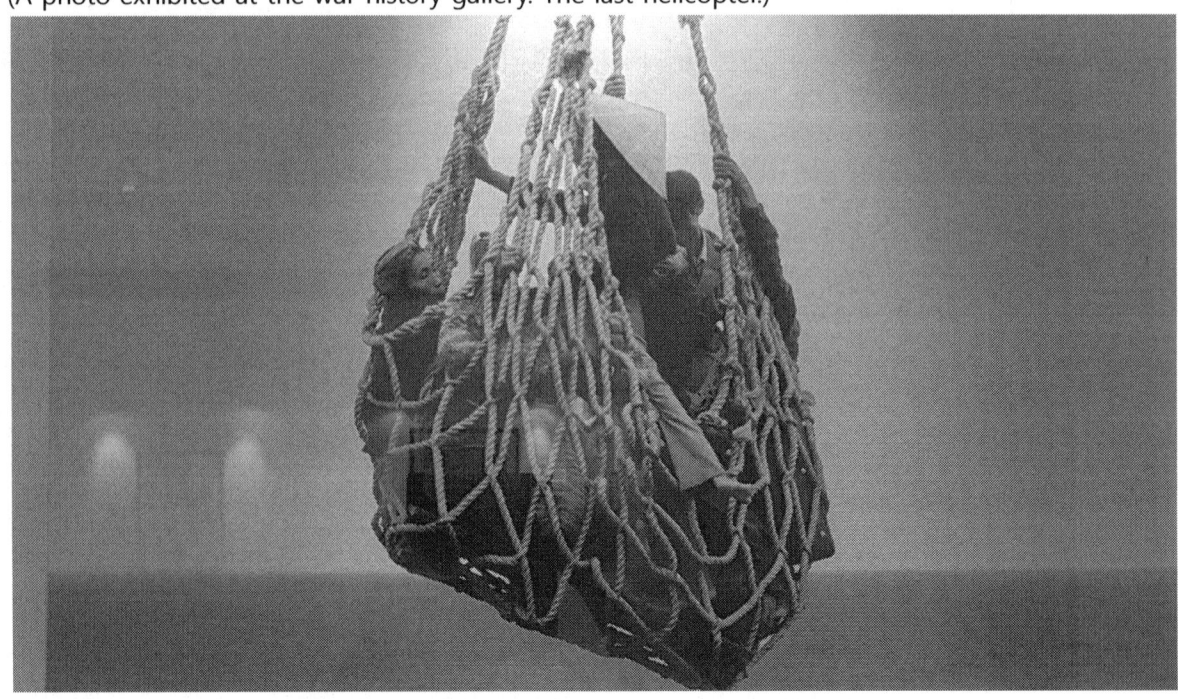

(Another photo showing the desperate escape.)

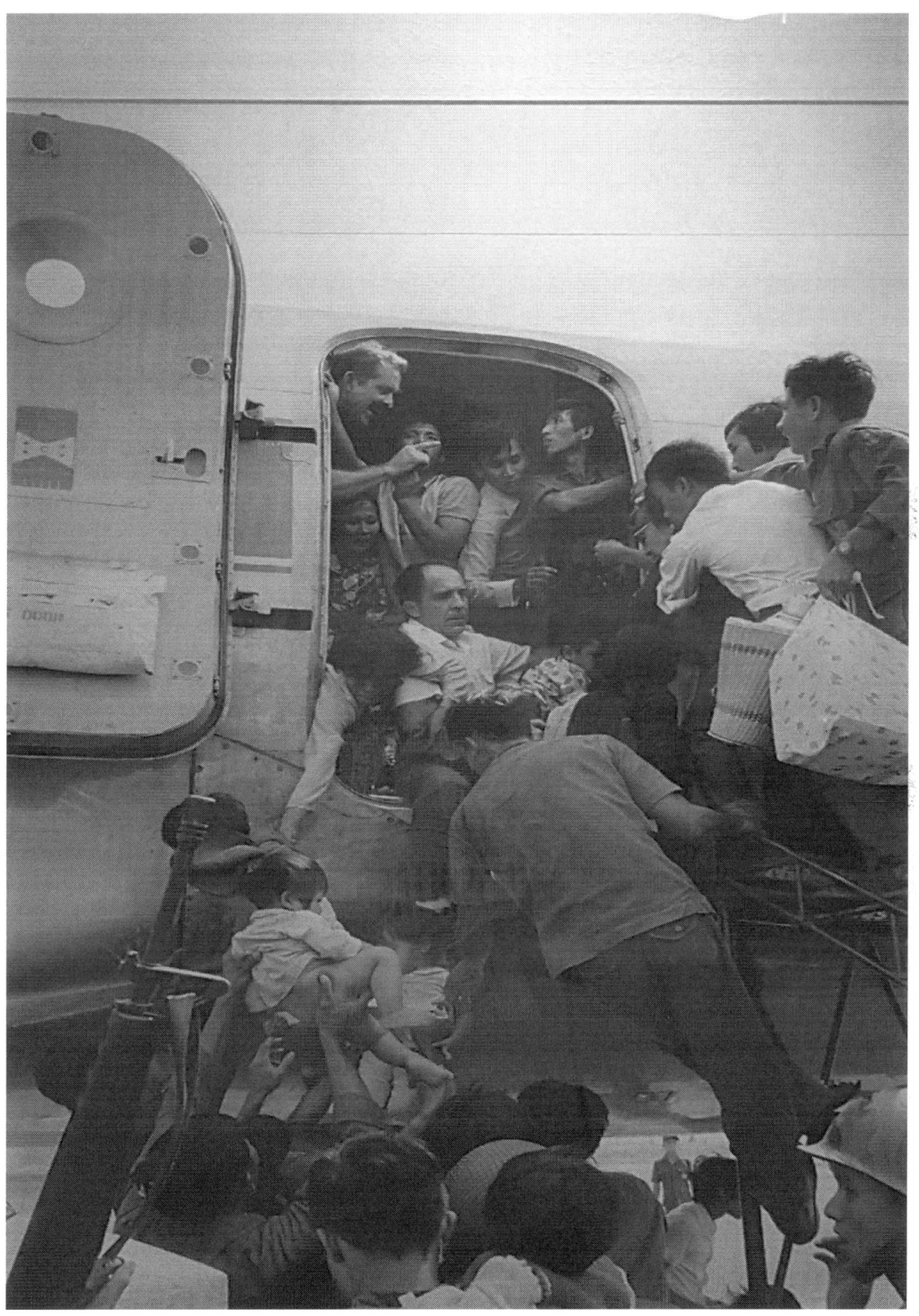

(Father tries to hand over a baby to its mother. Terrible.)

(You will meet "Opera House" at the end of this road of "Trang Tien". "Hotel Metropole Hanoi" is situated behind Citibank.)

(Hotel Metropole Hanoi)

(Opera House. Hilton Hotel is on the right.)

(Opera House & Hilton Hotel)

(Hanoi Stock Exchange (right). Hilton Hotel (left).)

(Hanoi Stock Exchange)

(Motorbikes are running on the street of "Ly Thai To" which is lying by the shopping mall of "Prada". A sign standing in front of the mall shows the name of the road.)

(Prada)

(A luxury watch, OMEGA (white), is standing on the street of "Ly Thai To". The rear door of Hotel Metropole Hanoi is on the other side of the road.)

(Hotel Metropole Hanoi. A small park is ahead.)

(After Hotel Metropole Hanoi, you will meet this small park. Early in the morning, people play badminton. At night, they exercise dancing at the park. Casa Italia is on the other side of the road.)

(Casa Italia. Italian Country Promotion Center.)

(From a small park behind Emperor Ly Thai To Statue, you are looking at National Bank of Vietnam. It is also near Casa Italia.)

(National Bank of Vietnam formerly known as Bank of Indochina.)

(4) Ho Chi Minh Mausoleum Complex

Ho Chi Minh Museum, House-on-Stilts where he lived until his final day, Ba Dinh Square where his Mausoleum is prepared are composed "Ho Chi Minh Mausoleum Complex". All are off on Mondays and Fridays. Before visiting, make sure the opening time of Mausoleum between 07:30 and 10:30 am only.

Ho Chi Minh Museum at Hanoi is quite different from the other museums with same name. It shows vast materials about his life in the beautiful exhibition halls. Be quiet when you take part in Mausoleum. He refused to enter Presidential Palace and stayed a humble house made of stilts until dying. You will come to know how much Vietnamese people respect him from the huge square of Ba Dinh which is prepared in front of the mausoleum. They call him "Bac Ho", Uncle Ho, instead of President Ho. Assembly Hall is also situated on the opposite side of the square.

Considering that you will meet museum after House-on-Stilts, you'd better pay a visit Ho Chi Minh's Mausoleum first. They prepare House-on-Stilts at the rear doors of mausoleum. When you come out of the house, you will automatically meet the museum. Therefore, your itinerary will be (1) Mausoleum, (2) House-on-Stilts and (3) Museum. For mausoleum, you have to deposit your bag and camera at the entrance..

(Ho Chi Minh's Mausoleum at Ba Dinh Square.)

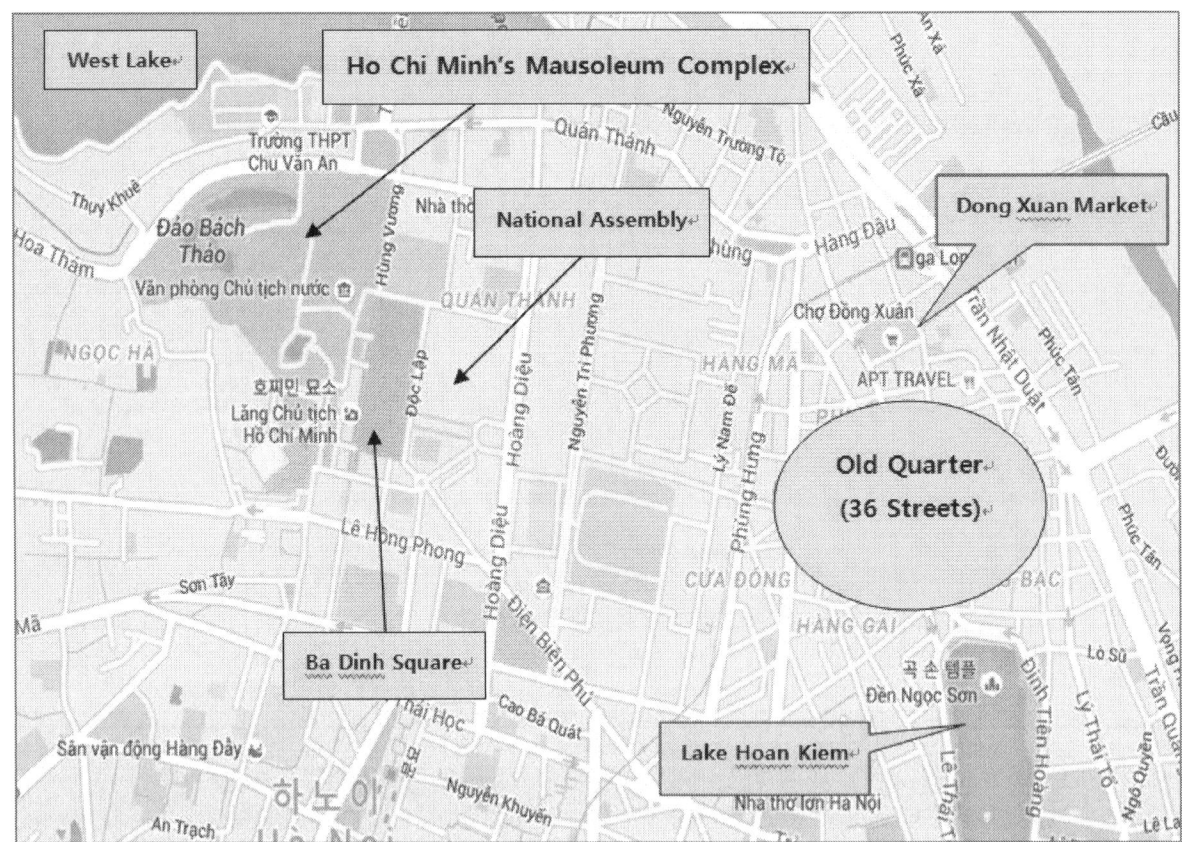

(Ho Chi Minh's Mausoleum Complex is quite far from Old Quarter. You'd better take a taxi. Around VND65,000 and 20 minutes.)

(Ho Chi Minh Museum)

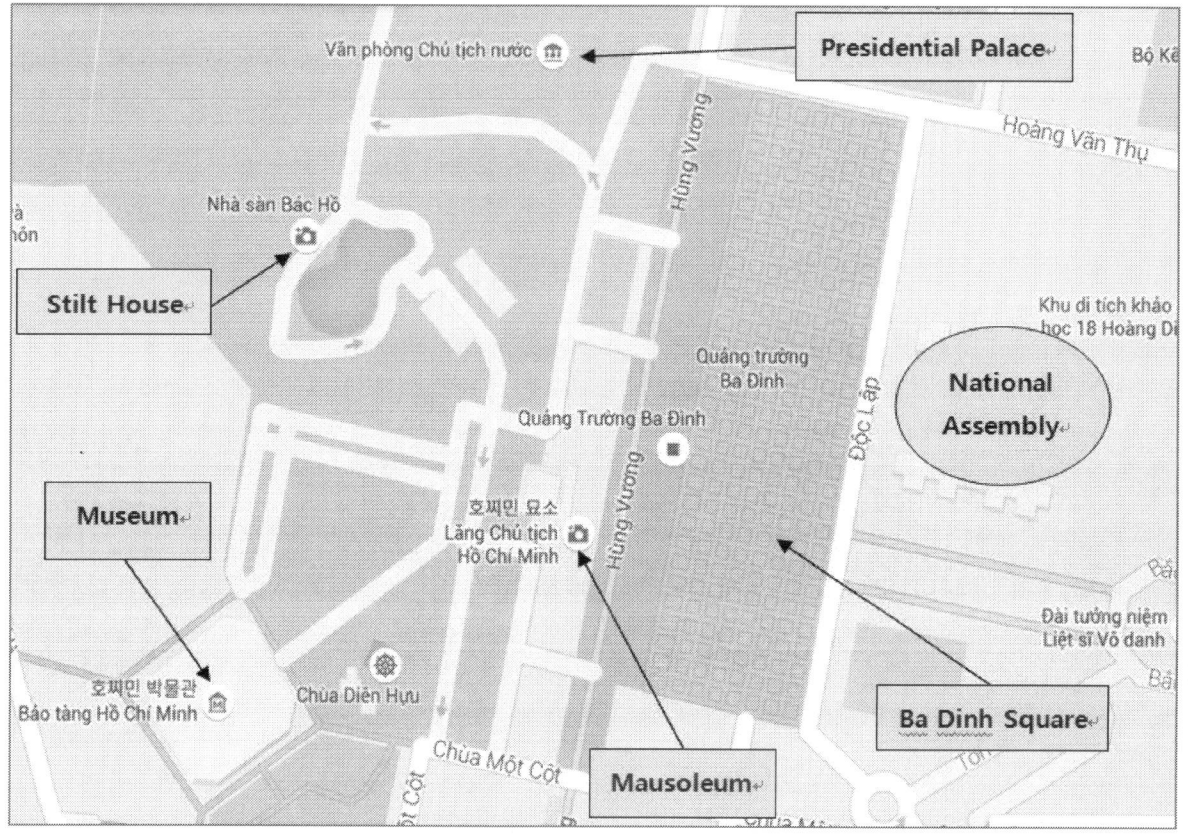

(Your itinerary at the complex will be made as follows.

(1) Go to the entrance to Mausoleum and deposit your bag and camera. Then, they will give you a custody certificate for your bag and a red bag with your camera.

(2) Deposit the red bag with your camera at the second office on the way to Mausoleum. They will give you another custody certificate for your camera.

(3) After mausoleum, get your camera back at the rear door of the mausoleum.

(4) Go to Ba Dinh Square before House-on-Stilts and take photos at the square as you want.

(5) House-on-Stilts at the cost of VND25,000.

(6) Museum at the same cost.

(7) Go to the entrance to Mausoleum again and present your first custody certificate to get your luggage back.

Now, let's go to "Ho Chi Minh's Mausoleum Complex".)

(4-1) Ho Chi Minh's Mausoleum

Ho Chi Minh (1890~1969) left his will to spread his ash on the 3 hills which are located at northern, middle and southern part of Vietnam. However, his will was not kept and his body has been kept in the Mausoleum at Ba Dinh Square after preservative treatment. Mondays and Fridays are off and open only between 07:30 and 10:30 am. Free admission. For the complex, show the photo below to taxi driver.

(You can get the main entrance of the Museum through this gate. However, for the Mausoleum, you have to go to the right from this gate instead of going through this gate.)

(Travelers are going to the right from the gate for the entrance to the Mausoleum.)

(Entrance to the Mausoleum is seen on the right.)

(At first, you have to deposit your bag and camera here. Then, they will give you a custody certificate and a red bag with your camera. Your camera in the red bag will be deposited at another office on the way to the Mausoleum at Ba Dinh Square. You will receive another custody certificate for your camera.)

(After depository, you will follow this long corridor until second depository for your camera. You can see Ho Chi Minh Museum on the left side of this corridor.)

(The Museum is on the left.)

(You are looking back at the first depository.)

(Ba Dinh Square. After the second depository, you will walk this pedestrian way shown in front. Ho Chi Minh's Mausoleum is partly seen on the left. They provide participants with a temporary corridor with a roof established on the pedestrian way and they take away the temporary corridor after 10:30 am.)

(Ba Dinh Square. The Mausoleum is standing on the left.)

(Ho Chi Minh's Mausoleum. Guards are always on duty.)

(Assembly Hall is situated on the opposite side of the Mausoleum.)

(You are looking back at Ho Chi Minh's Mausoleum on the way to House-on-Stilts.)

(After taking your camera back from the depository at the rear doors of the Mausoleum, you are walking to the entrance of "House-on-Stilts".)

(4-2) Ho Chi Minh's House-on-Stilts

Presidential Palace is located at Ho Chi Minh's Stilt House. He refused to move in the palace and stayed at House-on-Stilts from 1958 to his death on 2 September 1969. Presidential Palace has no owner yet.

House-on-Stilts is a traditional house of the mountain tribe which is built on stilts. Therefore, it looks like a 2 storied house. There preserved a table and 12 chairs on the ground floor. A simple bed and a table on the upper floor, tell you his philosophy on humble life. You will come to know the reason why Vietnamese respect him so much.

Mondays and Fridays are off and VND25,000 for entrance. Open at 08:00~11:00 am and 14:00~16:00 pm.

(Ho Chi Minh's Stilt House)

(After his Mausoleum, you will arrive automatically at the entrance to House-on-Stilts.)

(From Ba Dinh Square, you are looking at the entrance to House-on-Stilts.)

(VND25,000. Open at 08:00~11:00 am and 14:00~16:00 pm.)

(Take the left way for House-on-Stilts. Presidential Palace (yellow) is partly seen behind the park.)

(Presidential Palace (yellow) does not allow admission but you can take photos outside.)

(Way to Ho Chi Minh's House-on-Stilts.)

(A signboard standing on a forked road. The yellow house on the left is the house where Ho Chi Minh stayed between 1954 and 1958. For House-on-Stilts, take the way to the right.)

(Way to House-on-Stilts.)

(House-on-Stilts is partly seen by the lake.)

(For House-on-Stilts, go left and for Mango Road to the right.)

(Mango Road crowded with tall trees.)

(Way to House-on-Stilts.)

(The House-on-Stilts. He stayed here since 1958 until his final day in 1969.)

(One table and 12 chairs on the ground floor.)

(The upper floor. It is made of simple wood.)

(A table and a chair. It's all. How can I avoid respecting his humble life?)

(After taking a look at his house.)

(Guards are on alert.)

(Way out of the house.)

(The house he stayed between 1954 and 1958, is seen on the other side of the lake.)

(On the way to exit, you are looking back at House-on-Stilts behind the tall trees.)

(Convenient stores and souvenir shops at the exit.)

(Way to exit)

(Coming out of this exit, you will automatically meet the main entrance to Ho Chi Minh Museum.)

(4-3) Ho Chi Minh Museum

There are many Ho Chi Minh Museums in Vietnam. However, that in the Mausoleum Complex is quite different. At first, the exhibition halls of Ho Chi Minh Museum at Hanoi look like those of arts museum. And, countless materials on him are displayed in every hall. You will meet key communist philosophers like Karl Max and Lenin too.

Mondays and Fridays are off. Open at 08:00~11:30 am and 14:00~16:00 pm. VND25,000. Deposit your bag on the first floor and taking photos allowed.

(Main Entrance to Ho Chi Minh Museum. A Buddha temple is on the right.)

(Travelers are coming out of House-on-Stilts (front) and 3 people are going to the museum (left).)

(A sign for the "depository of luggage" is standing in front of the museum. When you are going to the depository to take back your bag, go to the left.)

("圓 覺 門", a temple, is situated on the right side of the entrance.)

(VND25,000. They call Ho Chi Minh as "Bac Ho", "Uncle Ho".)

(Exhibition hall.)

(The communist symbol with hammer and hook makes me back to the past.)

(A giant statue of Ho Chi Minh is standing at the entrance to the main exhibition halls.)

(A beautiful wooden sculpture welcomes you at the first exhibition hall.)

(A fantastic mirror hall.)

(Many old photos and pictures at the mirror hall.)

(Lenin at the mirror hall.)

(The second hall. It's so beautiful like an arts exhibition hall.)

(Ho Chi Minh in his young days.)

(Nguyen Ai Quoc is a name in his youth. This is taken in 1924. He looks very handsome.)

"DÙ MÀU DA CÓ KHÁC NHAU, TRÊN ĐỜI NÀY CHỈ CÓ HAI GIỐNG NGƯỜI: GIỐNG NGƯỜI BÓC LỘT VÀ GIỐNG NGƯỜI BỊ BÓC LỘT. MÀ CŨNG CHỈ CÓ MỘT MỐI TÌNH HỮU ÁI LÀ THẬT MÀ THÔI: TÌNH HỮU ÁI VÔ SẢN".

NGUYỄN ÁI QUỐC -1924.

"Malgré la multiplicité de couleurs, il n' y a que deux races dans l'univers: celle des exploiteurs et celle des exploités. Et il n'y a qu'une fraternité qui est vraie: la fraternité prolétarienne".

Nguyen Ai Quoc - 1924.

"Even though in this world people are from different races but there are only two group of them: exploiters and exploited. While there is only real fratern[ ] the fraternity of proletariats".

Nguyen Ai Quoc - 1924.

(It say that "Even though in this world people are from different races but there are only two groups of them : exploiters and exploited." Nguyen Ai Quoc – 1924.)

(Ho Chi Minh & letters)

(Artistic exhibition halls.)

(The exhibition hall looks like a gallery.)

(Who can imagine this is a museum for a historical man?)

(Take a photo with "Bac Ho", "Uncle Ho".)

(Way to depository to take back your luggage)

After Ho Chi Minh Museum, go to the depository to take back your bag. Follow the sign standing at the entrance to the museum.

(Go to the left as indicated by the sign for luggage. "Taking back vehicle and luggage".)

(You will meet this sculpture on the way to the depository.)

(Depository. Present the custody certificate and they will return your bag.)

("Return luggage". This windows are on the other side of the windows you have deposited the bag earlier.)

(After taking back your luggage, you may come out of the museum like the red arrow on the photo. People are going to the right for the depository before attending the Mausoleum.)

(5) Ha Long Bay

Ha Long Bay consists of around 2 thousand islands. It has been designated as a World Natural Heritage by UNESCO in 1994 and also chosen as one of the 7 World Natural Perspectives in 2011.

It takes around 4 hours by tour bus from Hanoi to Han Long Bay. Exactly speaking, to "Bai Chay Tourist Wharf" for the boats to Ha Long Bay. "Ha Long" is "下 龍" in Chinese which means "Descent of Dragon". According to a legend, a dragon came down from the sky to protect the enemy of Vietnam. The dragon vomited thousands of divine bead against the enemy and the magic beads transformed into islands on the sea later. It would be interesting to compare "Thang Long (昇 龍 Ascent of Dragon)", the original name of current Hanoi, with "Ha Long (下 龍 Descent of Dragon)" of Ha Long Bay.

Tour bus would be the best way from Hanoi to Ha Long Bay. They come to your hotel before 08:30 in the morning to pick you up and drop you near your hotel when return. Even considering 8 hours for a round trip to Ha Long Bay, one day tour would be enough. Compare price first between that suggested by your hotel and the price of travel agencies before booking. Except personal boat tour at Han Long Bay, it costs not more than US$30 including tour bus, boat, lunch and entrance fee to the cave.

(You have arrived at Ha Long Bay by boat from "Bai Chay Tourist Wharf". You can enjoy kayaking or another small boat tour for around 40 minutes at extra charge. It does not exceed US$3.00.)

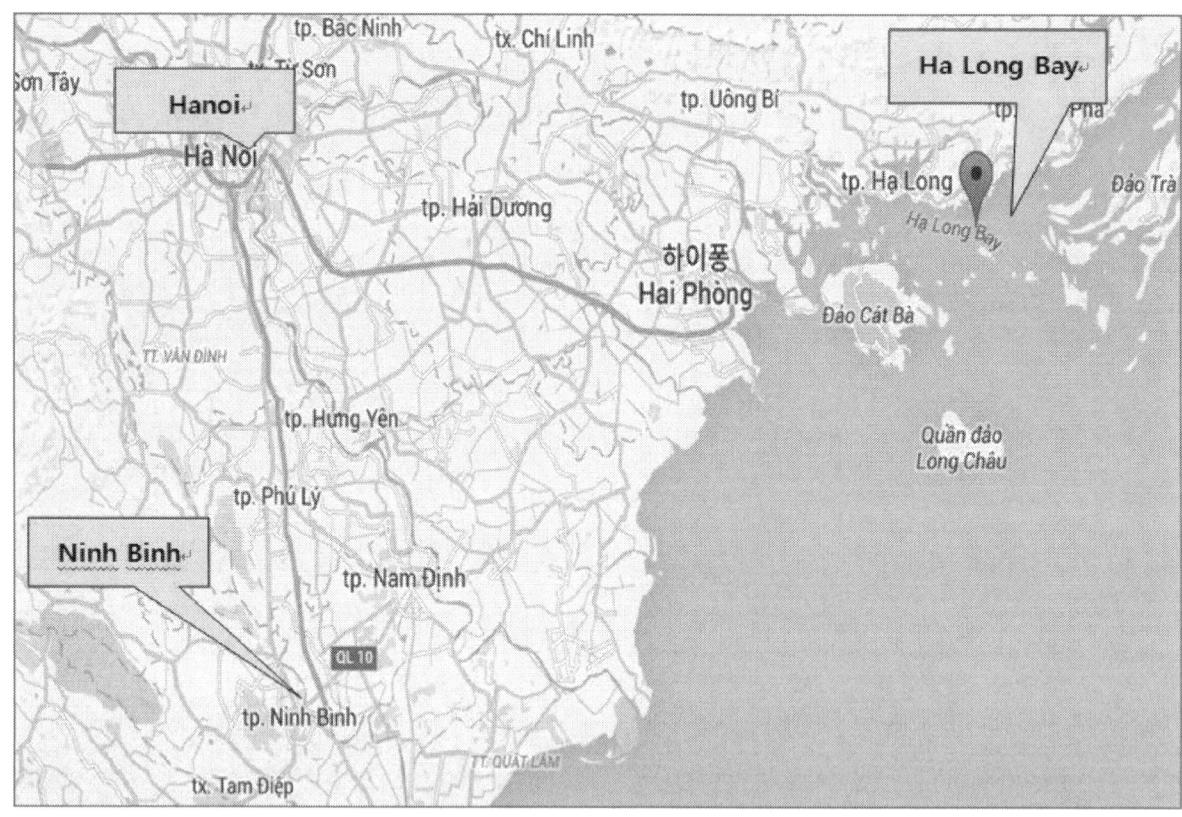

(It takes around 4 hours including 20 minutes break at a stopover. "Ninh Binh" at the bottom of the map, is called "Ha Long Bay" on the land.)

(Boats are waiting for you at "Bai Chay Tourist Wharf". Lunch will be served first when boarding. It's very delicious and enough. Now, let's start your fantastic journey from Old Quarter, Hanoi, to Ha Long Bay by tour bus.)

(Tour buses are waiting for travelers on the street of "Hang Bac" at Old Quarter early in the morning. Accommodation for 20 persons and cool with a guide speaking English well. They come to hotel before 08:30 a.m. to pick you up.)

(You are looking out of the window from the tour bus. It's normal for Vietnamese to have breakfast on the street.)

(In around 2 hours from Hanoi, you will arrive at a stopover. Take a 20-minute-break.)

(Shops, a convenient store and a restaurant. You will meet beautiful sculpture, jade jewelry and silk goods.)

(Various kinds of china are displayed in the shop of the stopover. They make all of these items by themselves.)

(Beautiful jade jewelry and pictures made by silk.)

(In around 2 hours from the stopover, you arrived at "Bai Chay Tourist Wharf".)

(Bai Chay Tourist Wharf. Boat quay is prepared on the other side of the entrance.)

(So many boats are anchored at "Bai Chay Tourist Wharf".)

(Way to boarding. Show the ticket you have received from the guide.)

(Tasty lunch would be prepared after boarding.)

(Tour boat)

(Clean tables are prepared in the boat. It has a toilet, too.)

(They sell water, beverages and beer.)

(Rice, vegetable, fish, clam, dumplings and chicken. A delicious and big lunch.)

(Upper deck. You can enjoy fantastic perspectives under the hot sun.)

(You've just arrived at Ha Long Bay. Here you can enjoy kayaking or boat tour for 40 minutes. It costs extra charge up to US$3.00. After taking a break, your boat will go to a cave.)

(Boats at Ha Long Bay are waiting for travelers.)

(Boat tour at Ha Long Bay.)

("Two-Humped Island". It's worth to be counted as one of the most beautiful islands of Ha Long Bay.)

(A stunning view of Ha Long Bay. Now, let's go to a fantastic cave.)

(Boats at the wharf for a cave.)

(Way to the cave.)

(Through the beautiful stairs.)

(You are looking down on the wharf you've passed through.)

(From the entrance to the cave, you are looking back at "Ha Long Bay".)

(At the beginning of the cave.)

(Travelers in the cave.)

(Cave with colorful lights.)

(Sometimes, it looks even weird.)

(There is a wide space at the bottom of the cave.)

(Beautiful stalactites in the cave.)

(Various kinds of stalactites.)

(After the cave, travelers are happy to take photos.)

(You will come back to "Bai Chay Tourist Wharf" to take tour bus. It will drop you near hotel.
When the guide says "goodbye" to all of you, do not forget to give a clap to him.)

(6) Ninh Binh

There are 2 attractions at Ninh Binh. One is "Tam Coc" and the other is "Hoa Lu".

When you travel Tam Coc by boat, you will come to know the reason why they call it "Ha Long Bay on the Land". The beautiful perspectives unveiled by the mountains on the river, will answer to your question. "Tam Coc" means "3 caves" and the boat will pass through the 3 caves.

"Hoa Lu" was a 42-year-long Ancient Capital of Vietnam until Emperor Ly Thai To moved the capital to "Thang Long (昇 龍)", i.e. Hanoi, in 1010. You will take a look at "Dinh Tien Hoang Temple" which was a royal shrine established by Emperor Dinh Tien Hoang. Can you remember that the name of a wide road running by the Lake Hoan Kiem near Old Quarter? It's "Dinh Tien Hoang Street". He reunified the northern Vietnam for the first time and established Dinh Dynasty. He designated "Hoa Lu" as its capital in 968.

It takes around 3 hours from Hanoi to Ninh Binh. One day tour for "Hoa Lu Ancient Capital" together with "Tam Coc", would be enough. It costs lower than US$30.00 except the tip of US$1.00 for the boat driver. Entrance fee to the shrine, lunch and boat fee are all included. Same as the tour to Ha Long Bay, the tour bus will come to your hotel before 08:30 in the morning. And, it will drop you near hotel when return.

(Boat tour at "Tam Coc". It takes around 1 hour for a round trip to 3 caves.)

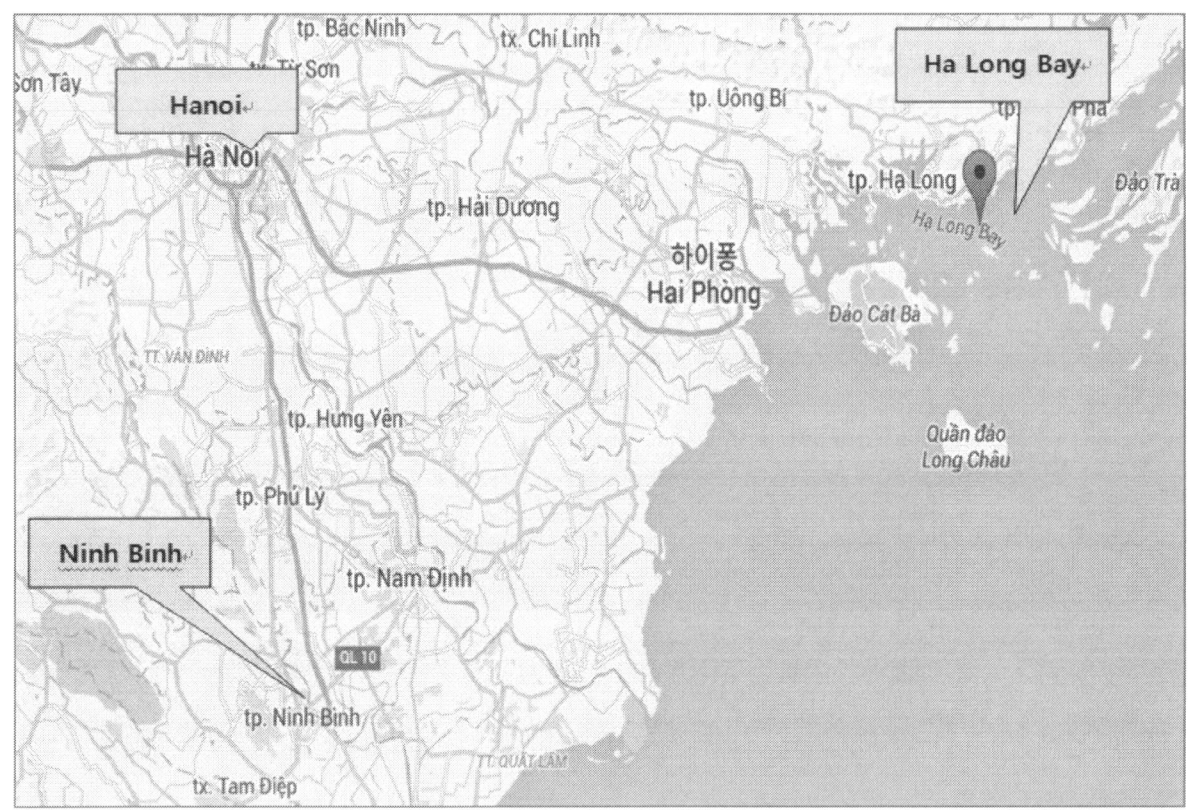

(It takes around 3 hours from Hanoi to "Hoa Lu Ancient Capital". After Hoa Lu, you will move to "Tam Coc".)

("Dinh Tien Hoang Temple" at Hoa Lu Ancient Capital.)

(A tour bus is waiting for travelers on the street of "Hang Bac" at Old Quarter.)

(In one and half hours, you will arrive at a stopover. They make beautiful silk pictures by hand.)

(You've just arrived at "Hoa Lu Ancient Capital".)

(Way to "Dinh Tien Hoang Temple".)

("東 門", East Gate)

(After the gate, you are going to "Dinh Tien Hoang Temple". The guide who speaks English very well, explains the history of Hoa Lu Ancient Capital.)

(Entrance to the shrine.)

(Way to the main temple.)

(Dinh Tien Hoang Temple. When you come into the shrine, you have to bend your back because the entrance to the shrine is too high to enter without a bow. It's the reason why they prepare the entrance too high.)

(Main shrine. Emperor Dinh Tien Hoang is in the middle and his 3 sons are surrounding him.)

(6-2) Tam Coc

After Hoa Lu Ancient Capital, you will move to Tam Coc. Having lunch at a buffet restaurant, boat tour will begin. It takes around 1 hour for a round trip to 3 caves. You may be surprised at the rowing skill by the boat driver. They row not by hand but by foot. When you leave the boat, do not forget US$1.00 tip.

(A buffet restaurant at Tam Coc.)

(A guide buys tickets for travelers. VND120,000 per person. Only 2 travelers on a boat.)

(Boat quay)

(They row by foot.)

(Splendid perspectives are unveiled.)

(To the first cave.)

(Watch your head.)

(Out of the cave.)

(Wonderful landscape.)

183

(On the river.)

(At the second cave.)

(Towards the last cave.)

(You will meet some boats selling beverages and fruit at turning point.)

(Way back to the boat quay.)

(Boats are coming and going back.)

(You come close to the boat quay. Near finish of 1 hour boat trip at Tam Coc. This is the end of your journey to Hanoi. Now, let's go to Da Nang, the biggest city in the middle area of Vietnam.)

Da Nang

(A long, long beach of "My Khe" at Da Nang.)

Contents

1. City Summary

Da Nang is the biggest city in the middle area of Vietnam. "Old Town" at Hoi An, designated as a World Heritage by UNESCO, can be easily accessed from Da Nang by bus.

Nearly almost of all attractions are located on both sides of the Han River, "Song Han" in Vietnamese. So many hotels, pubs, restaurants, travel agencies, museums, markets, key buildings are crowded near the road of "Bach Dang", which is well-prepared by the river. You can pay a visit almost of all attractions near "Bach Dang Road" on foot. When you are going to "Hoi An" for "Old Town", you can get there by bus at "Bach Dang Road"

If you cross the "Song Han Bridge", one of the most attractive bridges on the Han River, you will meet the beautiful beach of "My Khe" in 20 minutes. Therefore, you don't need to take a taxi in Da Nang except from and to airport.

(Da Nang is located in the middle area of Vietnam.)

(You are looking at the beautiful promenade well-prepared by the Han River ("Song Han"). This promenade goes along the street of "Bach Dang". "Brilliant Hotel" on the photo is standing on "Bach Dang Road".)

(You are looking at the "Song Han Bridge" from "Bach Dang Road".)

191

2. Public Transportation.

Taxi and bus are all. Except the way to Hoi An by bus, you have to use a taxi. However, you can pay a visit almost of all attractions even My Khe Beach on foot.

When you come out of the arrival hall from Da Nang Airport, take a taxi to your lodge at "Bach Dang Road". It costs around VND77,000 (equivalent to US$3.50) including toll fee of VND10,000. It takes about 20 minutes from the airport to Bach Dang Road.

When you go to "Old Town" at Hoi An, you can take a local bus no. 01 at the bus stand sitting just in front of Da Nang Cathedral, which is located near Bach Dang Road. It costs VND30,000 with extra charge of VND20,000 for a big luggage. You will arrive at Hoi An Bus Terminal in 1 hour.

(You've just arrived at "Da Nang International Airport". Different from the previous custom, you don't need to negotiate for the taxi fare, because taxies are running on the meter.)

(The bus stand for bus no. 01 bound for "Hoi An", which is located just in front of "Da Nang Cathedral". It takes around 1 hour from Da Nang To Hoi An Bus Terminal.)

(Da Nang Cathedral. Bus stand is on the right.)

3. Hotel

Except luxurious hotels such as Green Plaza Hotel, Novotel and Brilliant Hotel, there are so many cheap and clean hotels at Bach Dang Road. Here introduces a convenient hotel standing just by the street of Bach Dang. It's "Phuong Tam Hotel", which is located in the middle of the long "Bach Dang Road". From the hotel, you can get "Da Nang Cathedral" in 5 minutes on foot. Therefore, when you go to "Hoi An", you can easily take a bus no. 01. The beautiful "Song Han Bridge" is also accessible with 10-minute-stroll. The famous market of "Han" is located near "Phuong Tam Hotel", too.

("Phuong Tam Hotel" is standing on the street of "Bach Dang", where a motorbike is running.)

195

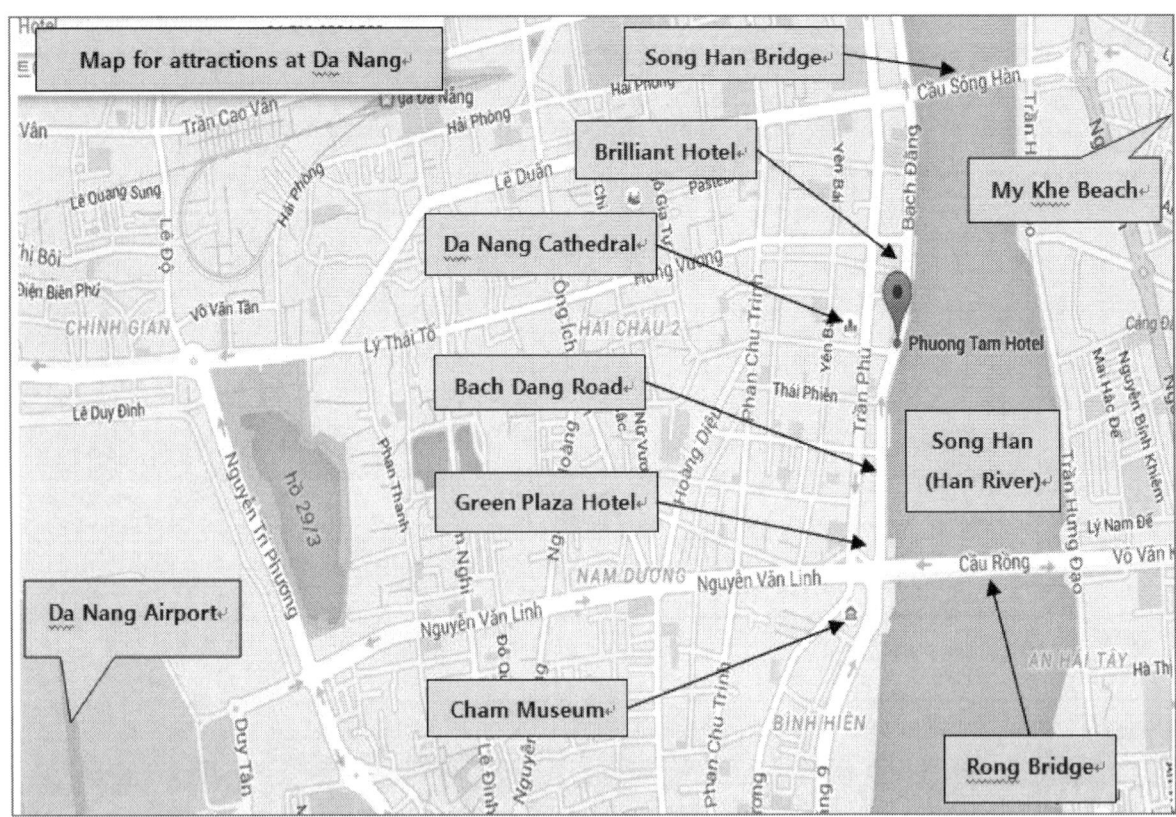

(Except "My Khe Beach", you can get almost of all attractions on foot from "Phuong Tam Hotel" which is indicated by a red mark on the map. Green Plaza Hotel and Brilliant Hotel are near the hotel.

"Da Nang Cathedral" is standing behind "Phuong Tam Hotel". "Song Han Bridge" on the upper side of the Han River and "Rong Bridge" on the lower part of the map are the most famous bridges built on the river. Even Cham Museum near "Rong Bridge" can be accessed on foot from the hotel. If you walk, you can also get "My Khe Beach" in around 40 minutes through "Song Han Bridge".

When you take a taxi at Da Nang Int'l Airport, it takes around 20 minutes and costs approximately VND77,000 including toll fee of VND10,000.)

("Pizza Pasta" is standing near "Phuong Tam Hotel". A black car is parking in front of the hotel.)

(Front Desk. Rooms are not so big but worth to be called as the best in cleanliness.)

(You are looking out of the window from the front desk of "Phuong Tam Hotel". A green taxi standing outside hotel is "Mailin Taxi", one of the famous taxies in Vietnam.)

(They deliver your breakfast to your room on the time you asked. Really tasty baguette, fried eggs, coffee, ginger tea and soy sauce.)

(Toilet is wide and clean. An excellent air-conditioner, a mini bar and free wifi.)

4. Attractions

As explained earlier, the street of "Bach Dang" by the "Han River" are crowded with hotels, pubs, restaurants, museums, travel agencies and markets. They call the river as "Song Han".

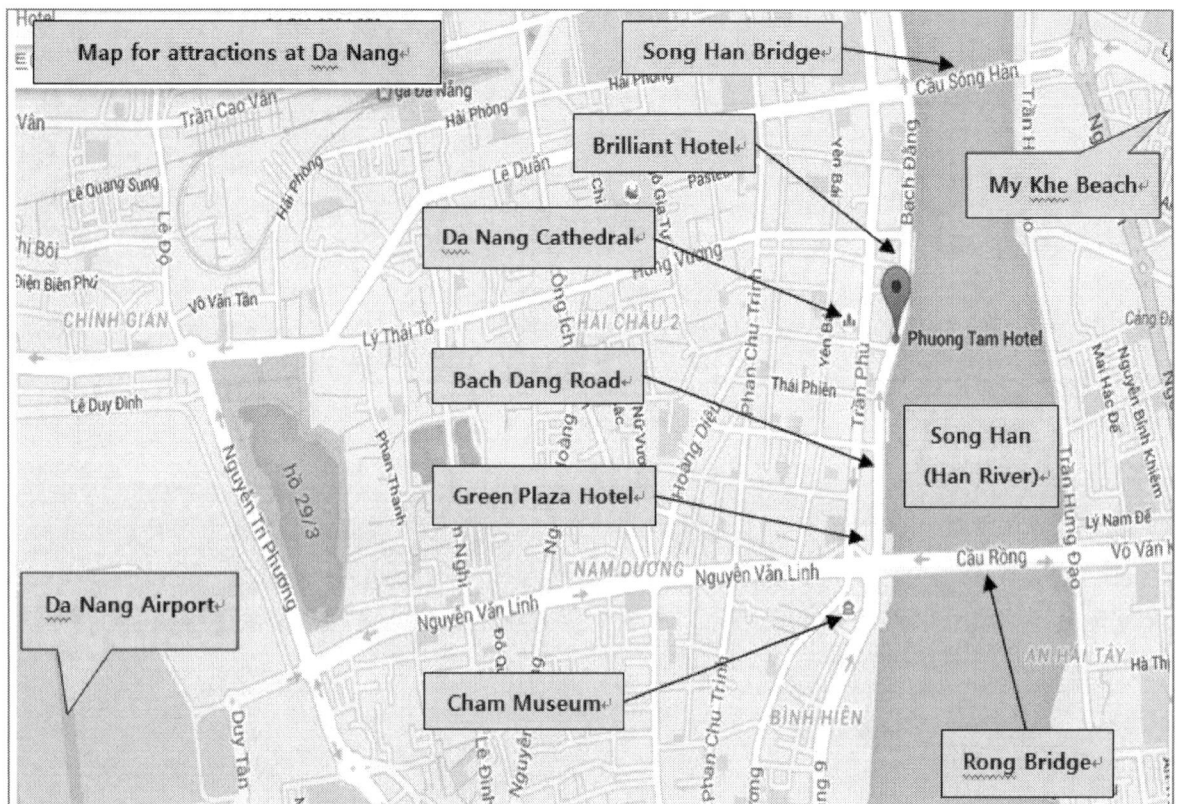

(When you come from airport to Bach Dang Road by taxi, you will meet the building of "Green Plaza Hotel" first standing at the entrance of the street. You will find "Rong Bridge", which means "Dragon Bridge", is on the right and a TV station is on your left. "Cham Museum" is located near the bridge.

If you walk on the "Song Han Bridge" lying on the upper side of the river, you can get the long beach of "My Khe" in around 30 minutes. When you stand on the opposite end of the bridge, you will find a 4-story-building on your right. It's "Vincom". Vincom has malls, a big food court, delicious restaurants and a beautiful theater of "CGV". "Da Nang Port" is also situated near the bridge, where you can enjoy one-hour-boat tour at night.

Here introduces "Bach Dang Road" first. And, (2) Da Nang Cathedral, (3) Cho Han (Han Market), (4) Song Han Promenade, (5) Song Han Bridge, (6) Vincom (CGV), (7) My Khe Beach, (8) Da Nang Port (Boat Quay) and (9) Charm Museum will be followed. (10) Old Town at Hoi An will be introduced at the finish.)

(A sign standing at "Bach Dang Road".)

(Travelers are taking photos on the "Song Han Bridge".)

(You are looking at "Da Nang Port". 2 giant buildings are standing behind the port. "Novotel" casting light from its head is standing on the right and "Da Nang Administrative Center" is standing next to Novotel.)

(1) Bach Dang Road

They call the street between "Rong Bridge (Dragon Bridge)" and "Song Han Bridge" as "Bach Dang Road". It is the best travelers' street. A TV station is standing at the mouth of the road. In addition to cheap hotels, luxurious hotels such as Green Plaza Hotel, Brilliant Hotel and Indochina Hotel are also located on the street. Only Novotel, a famous chain hotel, is standing by "Da Nang Port", where you will take a boat for one-hour-trip on the Han River at night.

(Bach Dang Road. "Phuong Tam Hotel" is located before "Brilliant Hotel" which is standing by the street on the photo.)

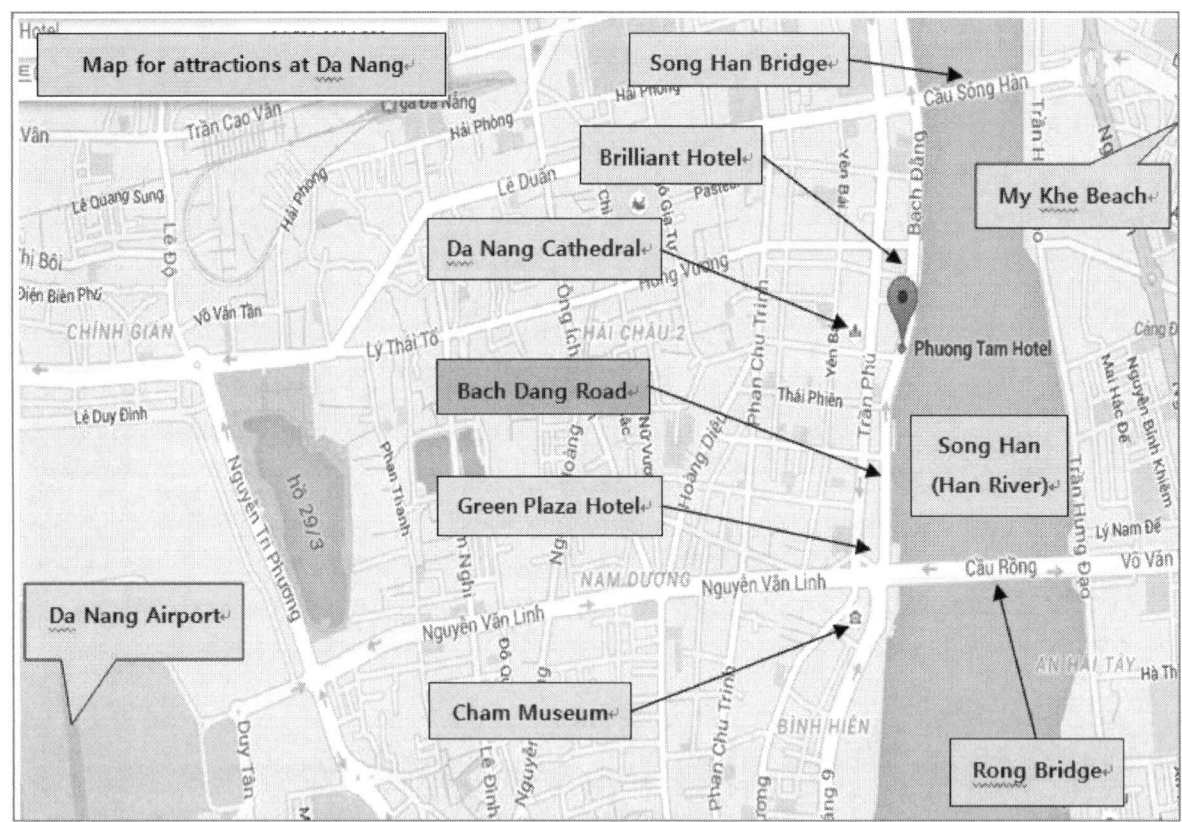

(Bach Dang Road begins at "Rong Bridge". You will also find "VANDA Hotel" standing high near Cham Museum.)

(You are looking at the mouth of "Bach Dang Road". A TV station is standing at the entrance and "Green Plaza Hotel" is standing behind the station. "Rong Bridge" is on the right where motorbikes are running to.)

(Motorbikes and cars are running on the "Rong Bridge". It means "Dragon Bridge".)

(Rong Bridge. "龍 橋" in Chinese and "Dragon Bridge" in English.)

(The mouth of Bach Dang Road is decorated with an arch. TV station is standing behind the arch and "Green Plaza Hotel" is partly seen on the very right.)

(You are looking at the long promenade well-prepared by the Han River. The street of "Bach Dang" on the left is running along the promenade The first building on the street is "Green Plaza Hotel". If you pass through the "Song Han Bridge", you will meet "Da Nang Port" before "Novotel".)

(You are looking at the yellow "Rong Bridge" seen behind the street of "Bach Dang", where motorbikes are running on.)

("Bach Dang Road" early in the morning. Vietnamese traditional houses are lined up by the street.)

(One of the tremendous cafes open by the "Bach Dang Road". If you take the road seen on the right, you will meet "Da Nang Cathedral" on your right in 3 minutes.)

(You are looking down on "Bach Dang Road" from the "Song Han Bridge".)

(Baskin Robins & Highlands Coffee.)

(Rather than daytime, even local people come to "Bach Dang Road" at night to take a rest with a cup of beer.)

(You are looking back down on "Bach Dang Road" from the "Song Han Bridge". The tallest building on the left is "Indochina Riverside Hotel (HSBC)" standing on the street.)

(You will meet shopping malls and a food court at "Indochina Riverside Hotel".)

(Shopping malls in "Indochina Riverside Tower".)

(Food Court)

(2) Da Nang Cathedral

From "Phuong Tam Hotel" at "Bach Dang Road", go around 100 meters to the right and you will meet a road to the right. Take the road and turn your eyes to the right at the first corner. Then, you will find "Da Nang Cathedral" standing on the opposite side of the road. A bus stand for no. 01 bound for "Hoi An" is located just in front of the cathedral. If fortunate, you can meet so many motorbikes at the cathedral when a mass is held.

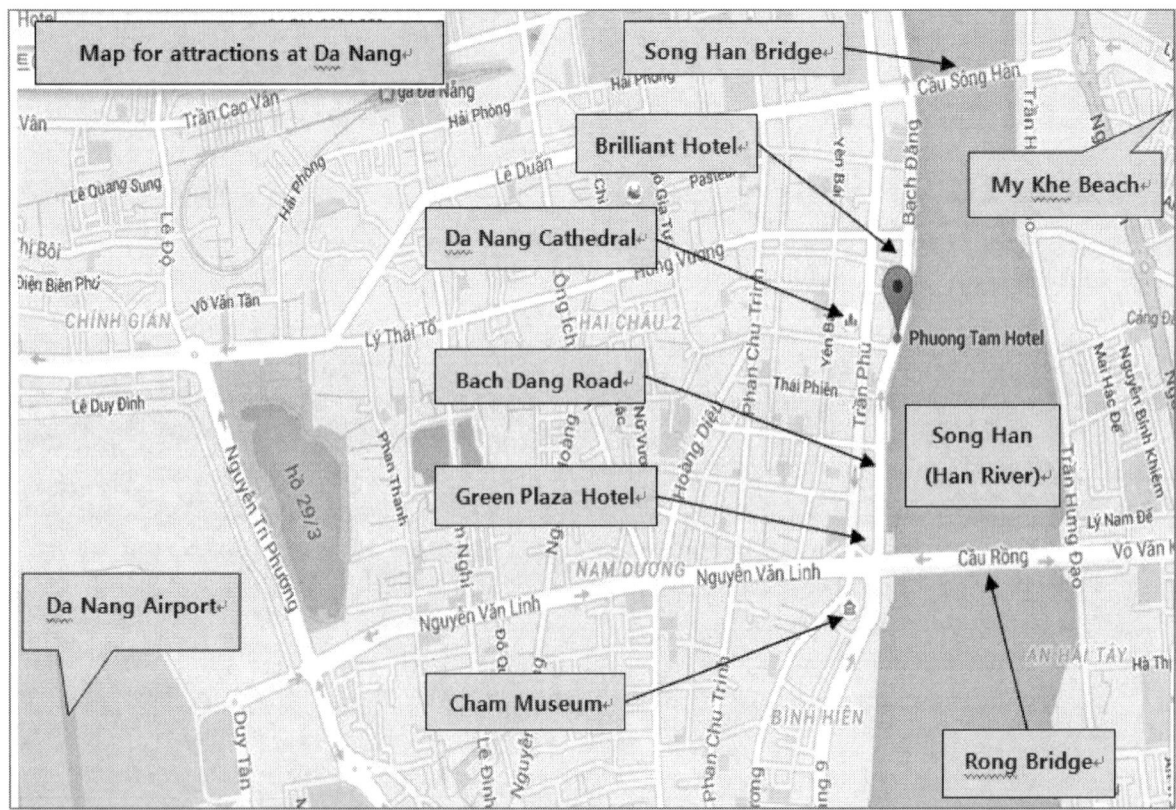

("Da Nang Cathedral" is located so closely to "Phuong Tam Hotel". You can get the cathedral from the hotel in 10 minutes on foot.)

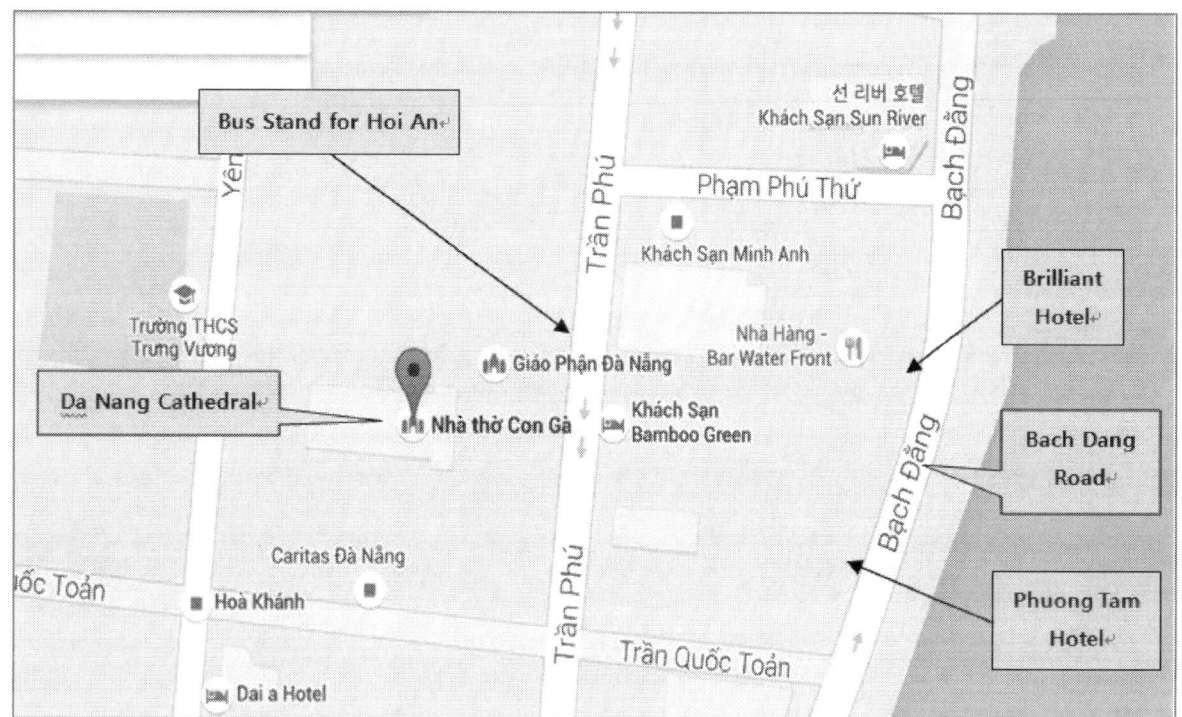

(An enlarged map for "Da Nang Cathedral". Brilliant Hotel and Phuong Tam Hotel are close to the cathedral.)

(It's time for a mass.)

(Another cathedral next to "Da Nang Cathedral".)

(A bus stand is prepared just in front of "Da Nang Cathedral". You can take a bus no. 01 bound for "Hoi An".)

(3) Cho Han (Han Market)

"Han Market" is a giant market at the street of "Bach Dang". You can get "Han Market" from Phuong Tam Hotel in 10 minutes on foot. They sell salted fish, raw meat, vegetable, fresh fruits and even foods.

(You are looking at the main entrance to "Cho Han", i.e. "Han Market".)

("Indochina Riverside Tower" is standing high behind "Cho Han", which is covered with red signs.)

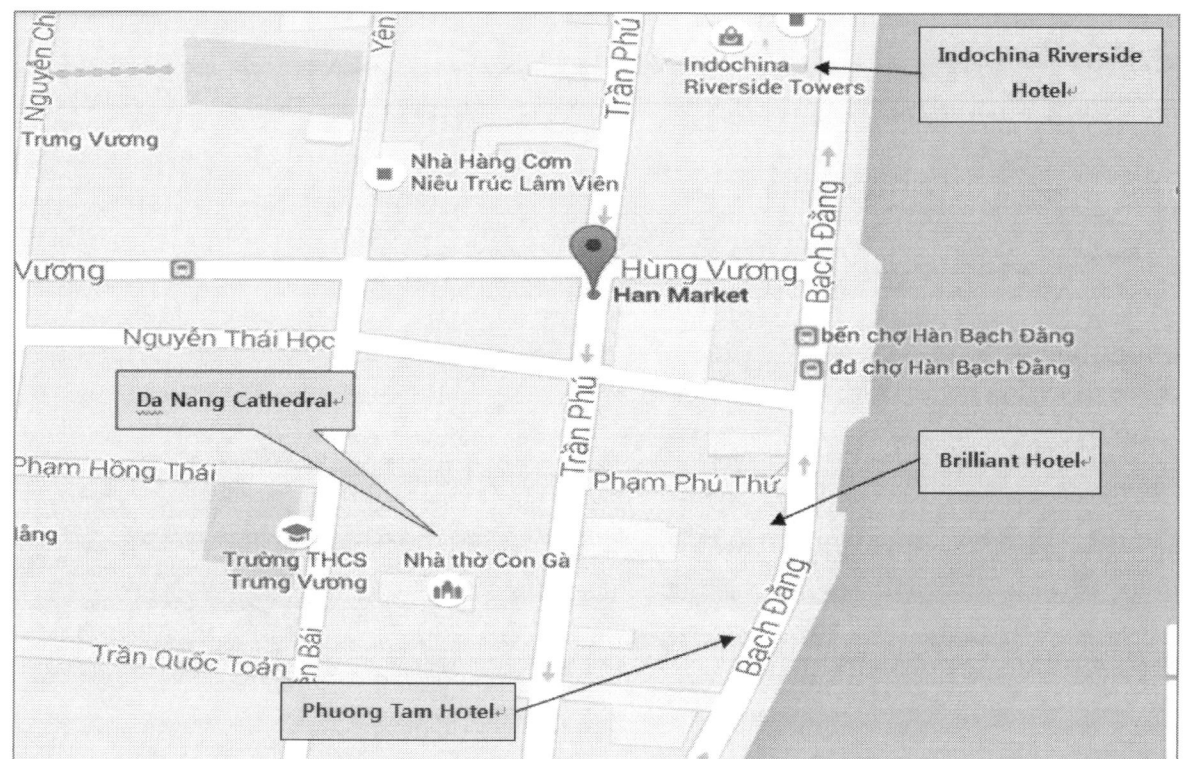

("Han Market" ("Cho Han") is located on the road of "Tran Phu", which is the same street where "Da Nang Cathedral" is standing. From Phuong Tam Hotel, go around 100 meters to the left and you will find the market on your left.)

("Han Market" covered by red signs is partly seen on the far left.)

(Way from "Bach Tam Road" to "Han Market" which is sitting on the right.)

(Around "Han Market".)

(Way to "Han Market")

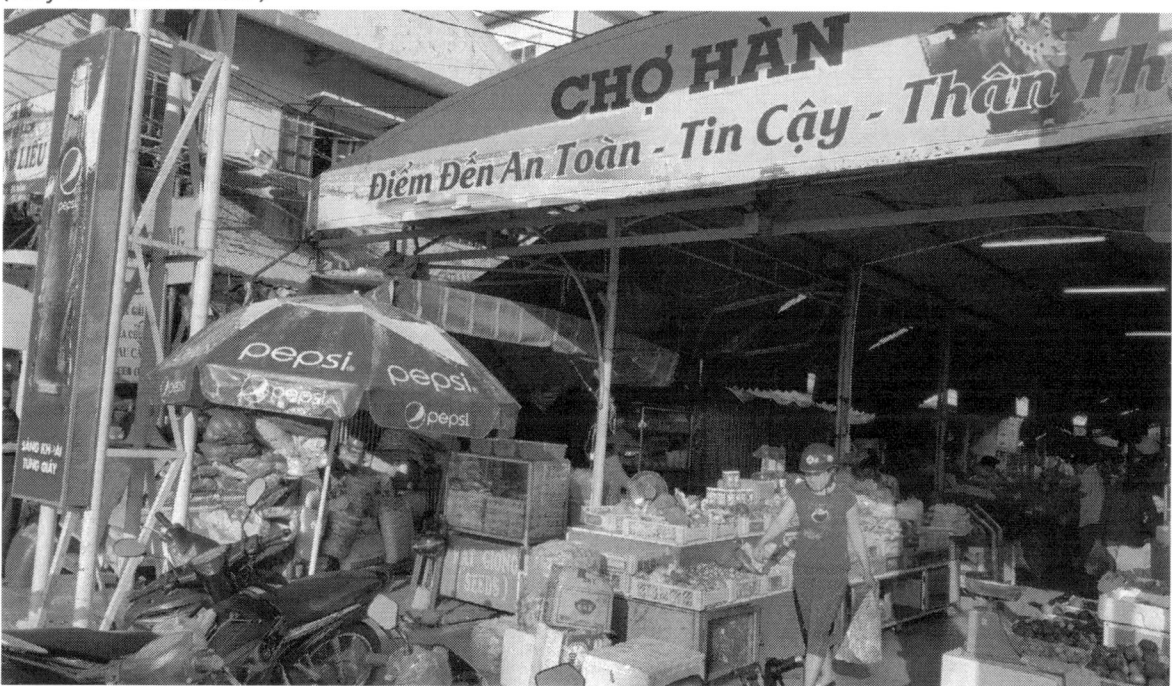

(If you come down a little more along the road of "Bach Dang", you will meet another market with the same name near "Cho Han".)

(You are going to "Han Market" standing on the right.)

(Inside "Cho Han". Abundant fresh vegetables and fruits.)

(There are so many shops selling various kinds of pickled fish in the market.)

(You can have a meal in the market.)

(There is a special area in the market for raw meats.)

(Outside market.)

(You are looking at "Han Market" from the street of "Tran Phu".)

(Han Market)

(Even condolence flowers, you can buy them at the market.)

(Go straight this road by "Han Market" and you will meet the street of "Bach Dang" shortly.)

(Han Market)

("Bach Dam Street" at the end of this road.)

(3) Song Han Promenade

"Song Han Promenade" is a long pedestrian way beautifully prepared by the Han River, i.e. "Song Han" in Vietnamese. It is a landmark at Da Nang. It goes really long from "Rong Bridge (Dragon Bridge)" until the last bridge of "Thuan Phoc" via the most beautiful one of "Song Han Bridge". When you pass through "Song Han Bridge" towards "Thuan Phuoc Bridge", you will meet "Da Nang Port" shortly. There you can take a boat trip at night.

If you take a stroll from the mouth of "Bach Dang Road" until the boat quay, it will take around 20 or 30 minutes. People are exercising at the beautiful promenade in the morning. If lucky, you can also meet a music performance at night.

(From the beginning of the promenade, you are looking at the way to "Song Han Bridge". The first building standing on the left, is "Green Plaza Hotel". The second one is "Brilliant Hotel" near "Phuong Tam Hotel", and the last one is "Indochina Riverside Tower". If you keep walking this promenade, you will meet the tallest building of "Novotel" after "Song Han Bridge". The hotel is standing on the left side of "Da Nang Port".)

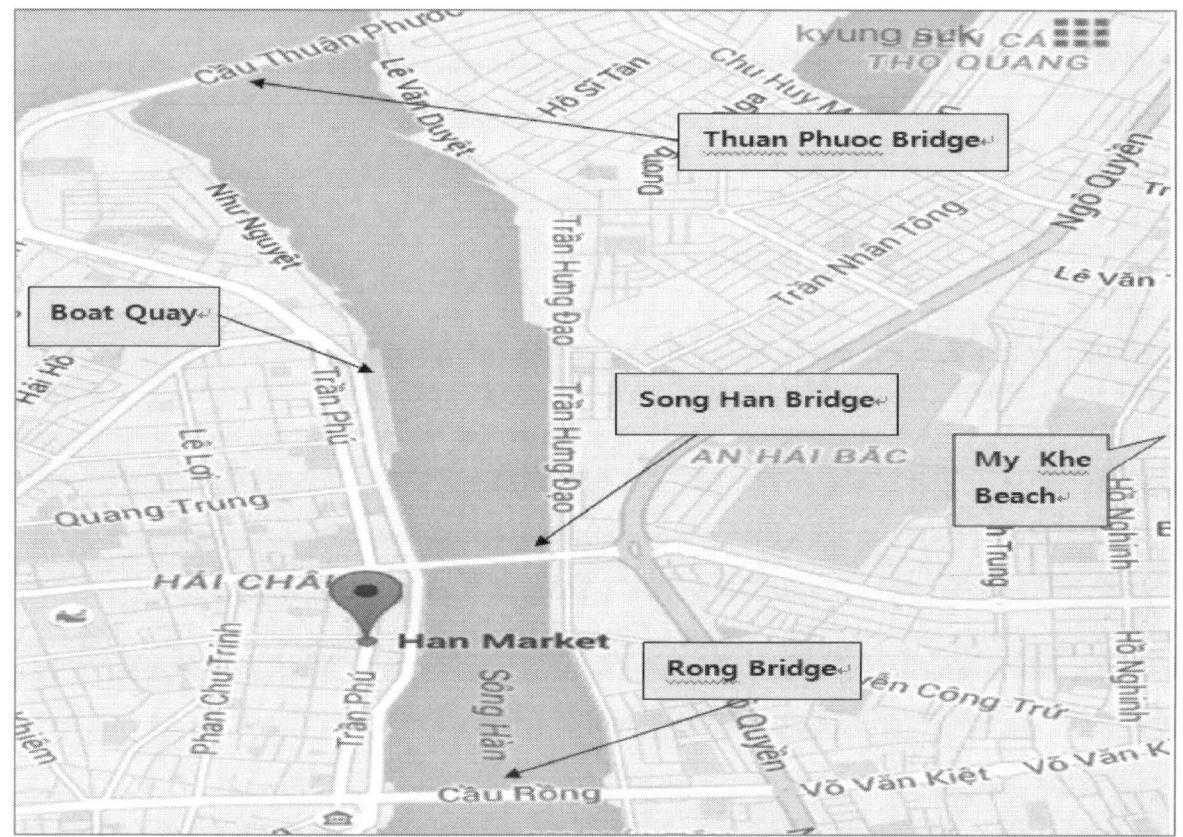

(After the bridge of "Song Han", you will find "Da Nang Port" which is stated as "Boat Quay" on the map. "Thuan Phuoc Bridge" is the final one built on the Han River.)

(From the mouth of the promenade, you are looking at "Rong Bridge".)

(You are standing at the mouth of the promenade.)

(People are taking a stroll in the morning.)

("Rong Bridge" from the promenade.)

(You are looking down on the riverside promenade from "Song Han Bridge".)

(Riverside Promenade goes along the street of "Bach Dang", where cars are running.)

(You are looking back at "Rong Bridge" (far left) from near "Song Han Bridge".)

(Riverside Promenade at night.)

(Light beams)

(Music performance at Riverside Promenade.)

(People are gathering more and more for the performance.)

("Song Han Bridge" lit the beautiful light.)

(Change color.)

(After "Song Han Bridge", you are going to "Da Nang Port". The house standing on the right is restaurant "Memory".)

(Restaurant "Memory")

(Restaurant "Memory" from "Song Han Bridge"".)

("Novotel" (right) is standing on the left side of "Da Nang Port". "Da Nang Administrative Center" is standing left next to "Novotel".)

("Da Nang Port (Boat Quay)" is seen behind trees.)

("Da Nang Port". You can enjoy a boat tour at night.)

(Many small boats are anchored behind "Harems 2 Cruise" seen in front. It costs VND100,000 for a boat tour and takes around 1 hour for a round trip on the Han River. Boarding begins from 7 pm.)

(Boats at "Da Nang Port".)

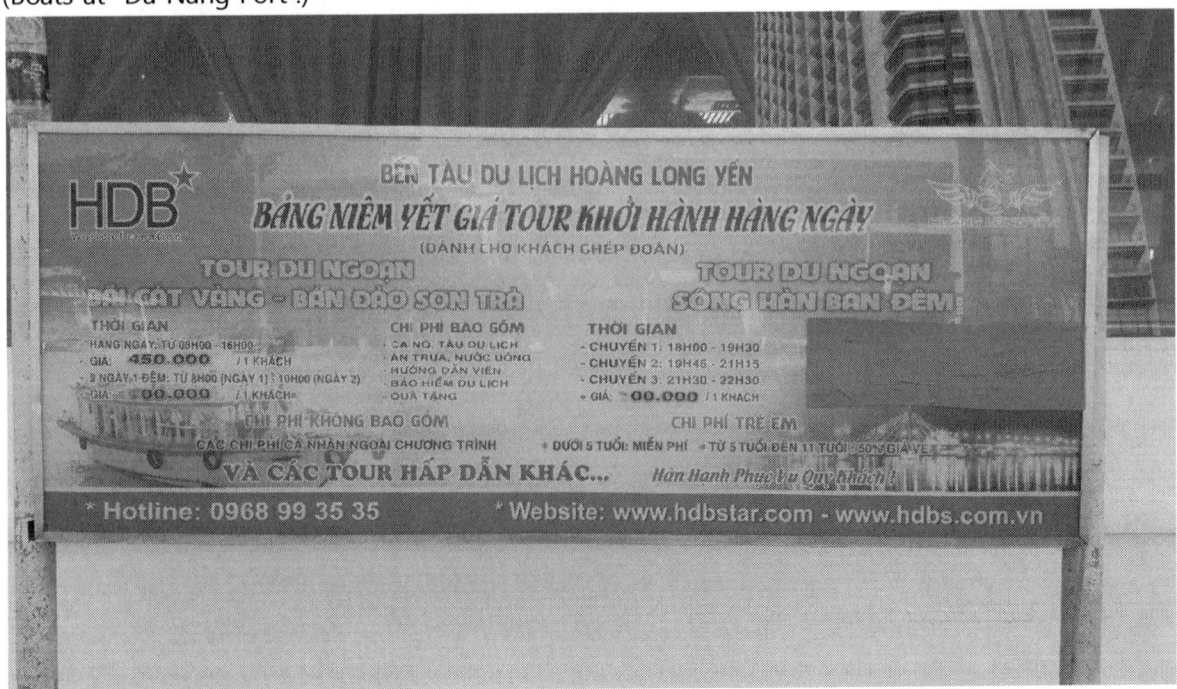

(An information board. All are stated only in Vietnamese. But you can catch the meaning.
www.hdbs.com.vn)

(Boats are waiting for passengers at night.)

(Take a seat on the upper floor.)

(Harems 2 Cruise.)

(People are taking a rest on the promenade near "Da Nang Port".)

(4) Song Han Bridge

They call the Han River as "Song Han". The most beautiful bridge on the river is "Song Han Bridge". Especially at night, you will meet so many travelers taking photos on the bridge. If try, you can also get the "My Khe Beach" through this bridge.

When you cross over the bridge from "Bach Dang Road", you will find a 4-story-building on your right. It's "Vincom". It has shopping malls, a good food court, a cinema theater named "CGV" and many tasty restaurants. It's a perfect place to take a rest on the way to "My Khe Beach". If you have dinner at "Vincom", you can take gorgeous photos on the way back to the street of "Bach Dang".

(You are crossing over "Song Han Bridge". "Vincom", a 4 storied building, is sitting by the tall building standing on the right. It's "Vinacapital Luxury Apartment".)

(From the Riverside Promenade, you are looking at "Song Han Bridge". "Vincom" on the far right, is sitting next to the tall building, "Vinacapital Luxury Apartment".)

(From the mouth of "Song Han Bridge", you are looking at the beautiful tower on the bridge.)

("Rong Bridge" is seen far away on the Han River.)

(From the bridge, you are looking down on the Riverside Promenade and Bach Dang Road.
"Indochina Riverside Tower" is standing tall on the right.)

(You are looking left. "Da Nang Administrative Center" (left) and Novotel are standing high near "Da Nang Port".)

(There is another promenade on the other side of "Song Han Bridge".)

(A vast rotary is sitting at the end of "Song Han Bridge". "Vincom" is on the right. If you walk along the left road from the rotary, you will arrive at "My Khe Beach" in around 20 minutes. It's "Pham Van Dong Road".)

(Vincom. malls, a food court, a cinema theater and restaurants.)

(From the rotary, you are looking back at "Song Han Bridge".)

(From Vincom, you are looking at "Song Han Bridge".)

(Changed color.)

("Song Han Bridge" on the way back to "Bach Dang Road".)

(On "Song Han Bridge", you are looking down on the gorgeous restaurant of "Memory" on the far left. "Da Nang Administrative Center" (left) and Novotel are standing tall behind "Da Nang Port".)

(Restaurant "Memory".)

("Rong Bridge" from "Song Han Bridge".)

("Song Han Bridge" from "Da Nang Port".)

(5) Vincom (CGV)

When you cross over "Song Han Bridge", you will meet "Vincom" on the right. The 4 storied building has shopping malls, a big supermarket, a food court, a movie theater (CGV) and tasty restaurants. After swimming at "My Khe Beach", have a dinner here and cross over the bridge back to "Bach Dang Road". Then, you can take fantastic photos of the Han River at night.

(At the other end of "Song Han Bridge", you can easily find "Vincom" on your right.)

(Vincom at night.)

(Shopping malls at Vincom.)

("Vinmart", one of the famous supermarkets in Vietnam. Keep your bag at depository first before entering.)

(Restaurants at the 4th floor.)

(There is an ice rink behind "Coffee Station" (photo) prepared at the center of the 4th floor.)

("Mochi Sweets" and "Jollibee" at the end of the escalator to the 4th floor.)

("Mochi Sweets")

(Food Court)

(Food Court. Various kinds of food from the world.)

(Restaurants. "GoGi", a Korean BBQ restaurant (left), and "Crystal Jade", a Chinese restaurant (right). "CGV", a movie theatre, is located on the opposite side of the Chinese restaurant.)

(A cinema theater, "CGV".)

(Ticket Box)

(Rest area at "CGV".)

(Ice rink)

(You are looking outside "Vincom".)

(7) My Khe Beach

It has really long sands. It takes around 20 meters on foot from "Vincom" to "My Khe Beach". When you stand in front of "Vincom" with your back to the mall, cross the road straight and take the wide road to the right. It's "Pham Van Dong Road". "My Khe Beach" is situated at the end of the street.

(A "just married" couple is taking photos at "My Khe Beach")

(My Khe Beach (right side)

(A convenient store (right) and parasols on the beach.)

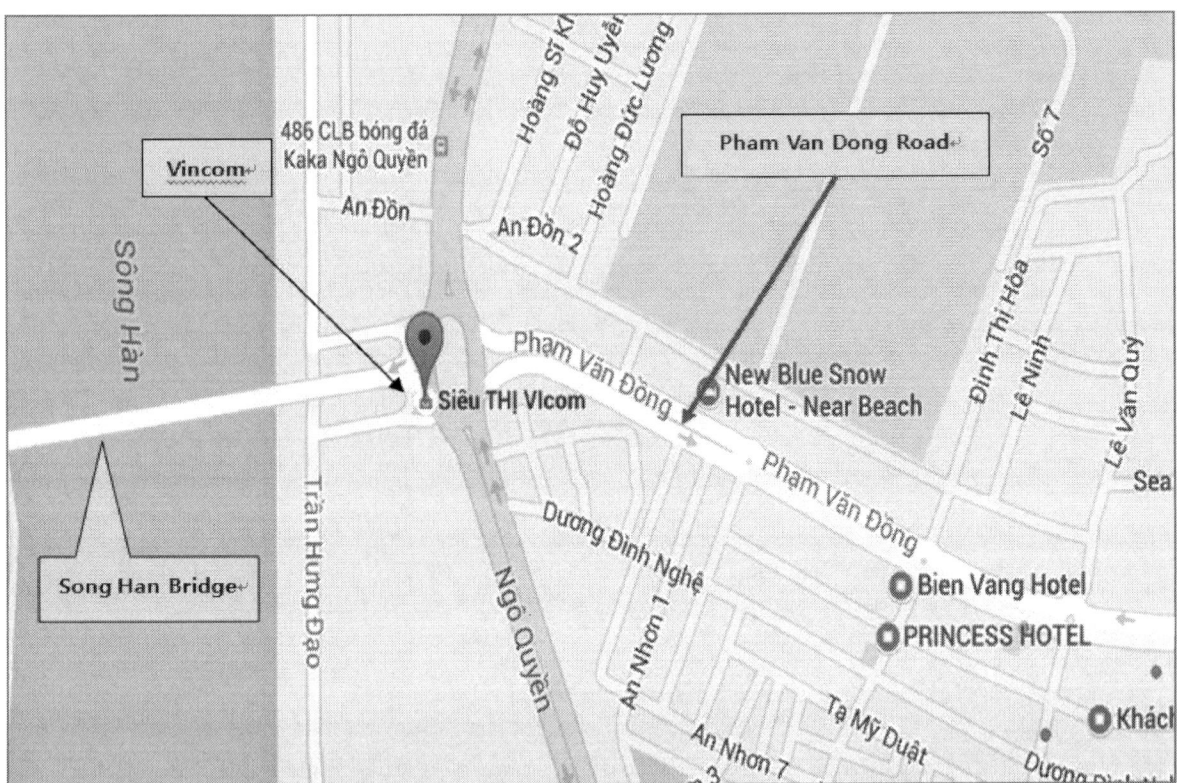

(Stand with your back to "Vincom" and cross the road straight. Take the way to the right. It's "Pham Van Dong Road". Keep walking along the street of "Pham Van Dong" and you will meet "My Khe Beach" at the end of the road in around 20 minutes.)

(From "Vincom", cross this road straight and take the way to the right. It's "Pham Van Dong Road".)

(You are looking back at "Vincom" on the crosswalk.)

(After crossing the road, you are looking at a motorbike running towards "Pham Van Dong Road".)

(The beginning of "Pham Van Dong Road".)

(Pham Van Dong Road. Keep walking straight until the end of this road. Then, you will meet "My Khe Beach" in around 20 minutes.)

(A sign standing on "Pham Van Dong Road".)

(Cafe "102" on Pham Van Dong Road.)

("My Khe Beach" is situated at the end of this road.)

(My Khe Beach)

(Speed boat)

(My Khe Beach. Endless sands.)

(My Khe Beach)

(A restroom is seen behind the beach parasols.)

(Shower place is prepared in front of the toilet which is seen far right on the photo.)

(8) Da Nang Port

"Da Nang Port", i.e. boat quay, is located near "Novotel", which is standing tall next to the other skyscraper, "Da Nang Administrative Center". Boat tour for 1 hour begins at 7 pm. VND100,000.

("Da Nang Port". Boats are anchored behind the cruise.)

(Boats are waiting for travelers at "Da Nang Port".)

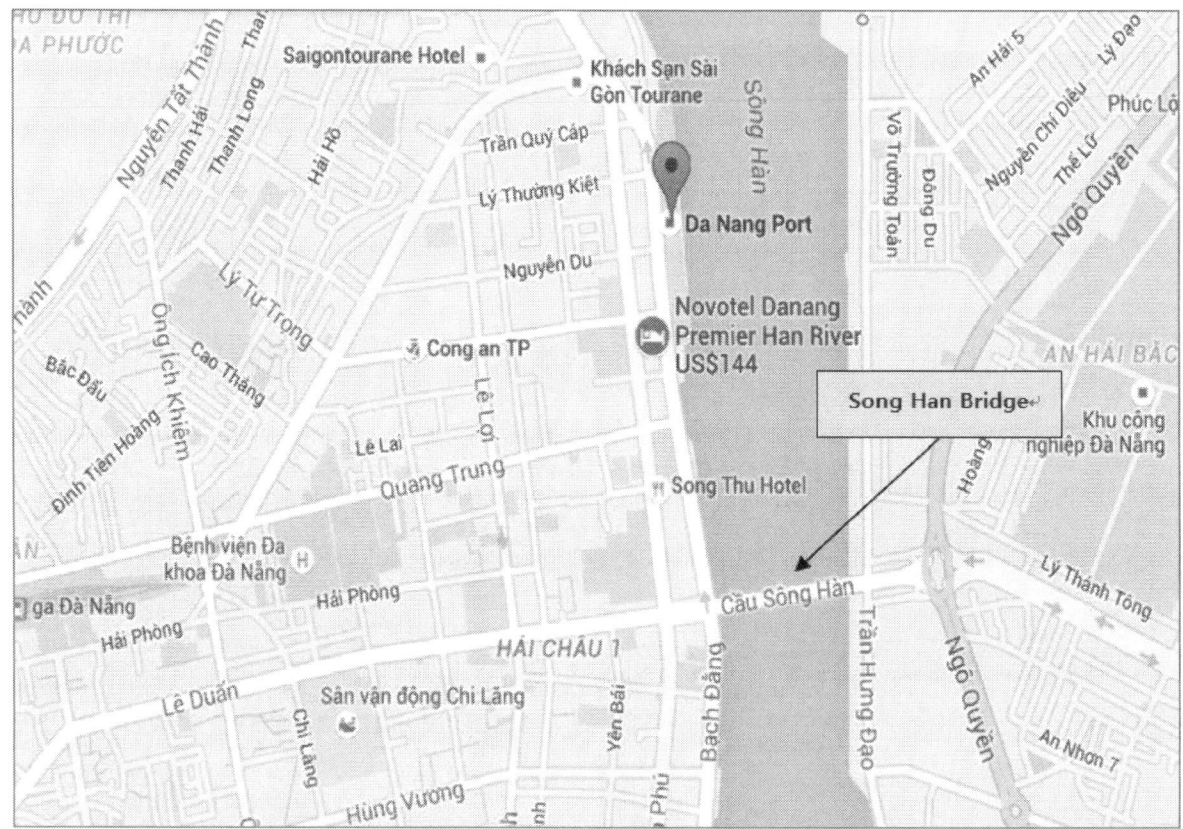

(Keep walking along the promenade by the Han River and you will meet "Da Nang Port" after "Song Han Bridge". 2 skyscrapers, "Novotel and "Da Nang Administrative Center", are standing tall near the boat quay.)

(After Song Han Bridge, you are going to "Da Nang Port", which is partly seen on the right. "Da Nang Administrative Center (left)" and "Novotel" are standing on the left.)

269

(Novotel)

(Da Nang Administrative Center)

(Tour boats are behind "Harems 2 Cruise" seen on the photo.)

("Harems 2 Cruise" at night.)

(Tour boats. VND100,000 for 1 hour.)

(Tour boats at "Da Nang Port".)

(Take a seat on the upper deck.)

(Wait until all seats are occupied.)

(A dragon boat is sailing on the Han River.)

(From a boat, you are looking at restaurant "Memory" by the Han River.)

("Da Nang Administrative Center (left)" and "Novotel" are standing behind restaurant "Memory".
"Thuan Phuoc Bridge", the last one on the Han River, is seen far away to the right.)

(You are looking at "Bach Dang Road".)

(Rong Bridge)

(A boat is sailing on the Han River.)

(A Merlion standing on the other side of the river, spouts water.)

(There are so many pedestrians on the other promenade.)

278

(Song Han Bridge)

(Song Han Bridge)

(9) Charm Museum

Champa Kingdom, an ancient kingdom thrived in the middle area of Vienam, believed in Hindu Gods. Charm Museum displays so many stone sculptures found in the area. It's very easy to get the museum from Bach Dang Road, because it is situated at the rotary near the mouth of the street. A giant hotel of "VANDA" is standing tall near the museum and "Rong Bridge" is also lying by "Charm Museum". Admission fee is VND40,000.

(From the entrance to the street of "Bach Dang", you are looking at "Charm Museum".)

("VANDA Hotel" is standing near the museum.)

(Entrance to Cham Museum.)

(From "Cham Museum", you are looking at the mouth of "Bach Dang Road". Motorbikes are running towards "Rong Bridge". A TV Station is partly seen on the very left.)

(Ticket Office. VND40,000.)

(Start from the left chamber.)

(Exhibition hall. Various kinds of Hindu gods.)

(Demigods)

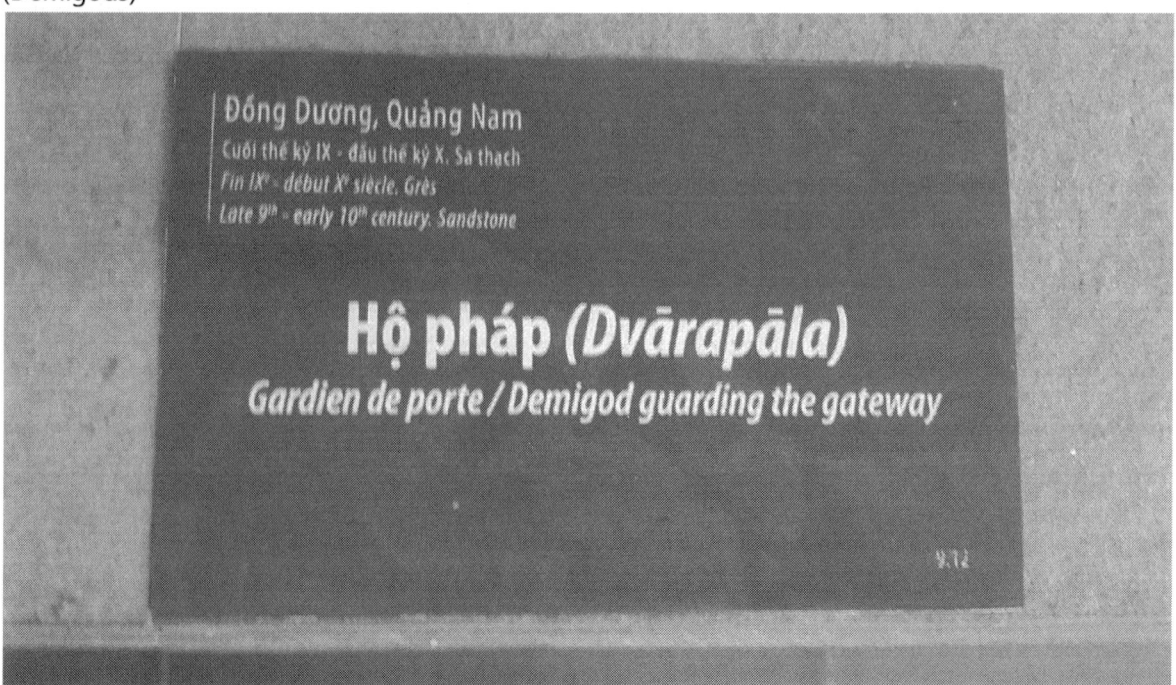

(Information plate. "Demigod guarding the gateway".)

(God Brahma, the utmost god in Hinduism. God of Creation. There are 3 most important gods in Hinduism. They are Brahma, Vishnu and Siva.)

(God Vishnu, the other one of the 3 key gods. God of Maintenance.)

(God Siva, one of the 3 most important gods. God of Demolition.)

(Buddha)

(10) Hoi An ("Old Town")

"Old Town" at Hoi An has been designated as World Cultural Heritage by UNESCO. You can pay a visit "Old Town" by bus at Da Nang. Take a bus no. 01 at the bus stand sitting in front of "Da Nang Cathedral" and you will arrive at "Hoi An Bus Terminal" in around 1 hour.

A ticket to the town costs VND120,000 as of July 2015. You can use the ticket for 3 days. 2 or 3 hours would be enough to take a stroll in the town. Therefore, if you leave Da Nang before 8 am, you can come back at the same day.

("Old Town" at Hoi An. You have to buy another ticket for "Cantonese Assembly Hall" seen on the right. Now, let's go to the bus stand in front of "Da Nang Cathedral".)

(Bus tand at "Da Nang Cathedral")

As explained earlier, "Da Nang Cathedral" takes around 5 minutes on foot from "Phuong Tam Hotel" at "Bach Dang Road". The bus stand for No. 01 bound for "Hoi An" is located just in front of the cathedral. The final stop of the bus is "Hoi An Bus Terminal". It costs VND30,000 and extra VND20,000 when you have a big luggage. It takes around 1 hours to the terminal.

(Da Nang Cathedral. Bus stand is on the right.)

(Bus stand in front of Da Nang Cathedral.)

(A yellow bus no. 01 is approaching the bus stand. VND30,000 and additional VND20,000 in case of a big luggage.)

(Cheap but a little hot inside.)

(You've just arrived at "Hoi An Bus Terminal".)

(Way from "Hoi An Bus Terminal" to "Old Town")

Here shows you 2 maps. First one is for the direction you have to take when you come out of the terminal. The second one will show you the way to "Old Town" from a crossroads you will meet in 10 minutes from the terminal. Here shows you the first one below.

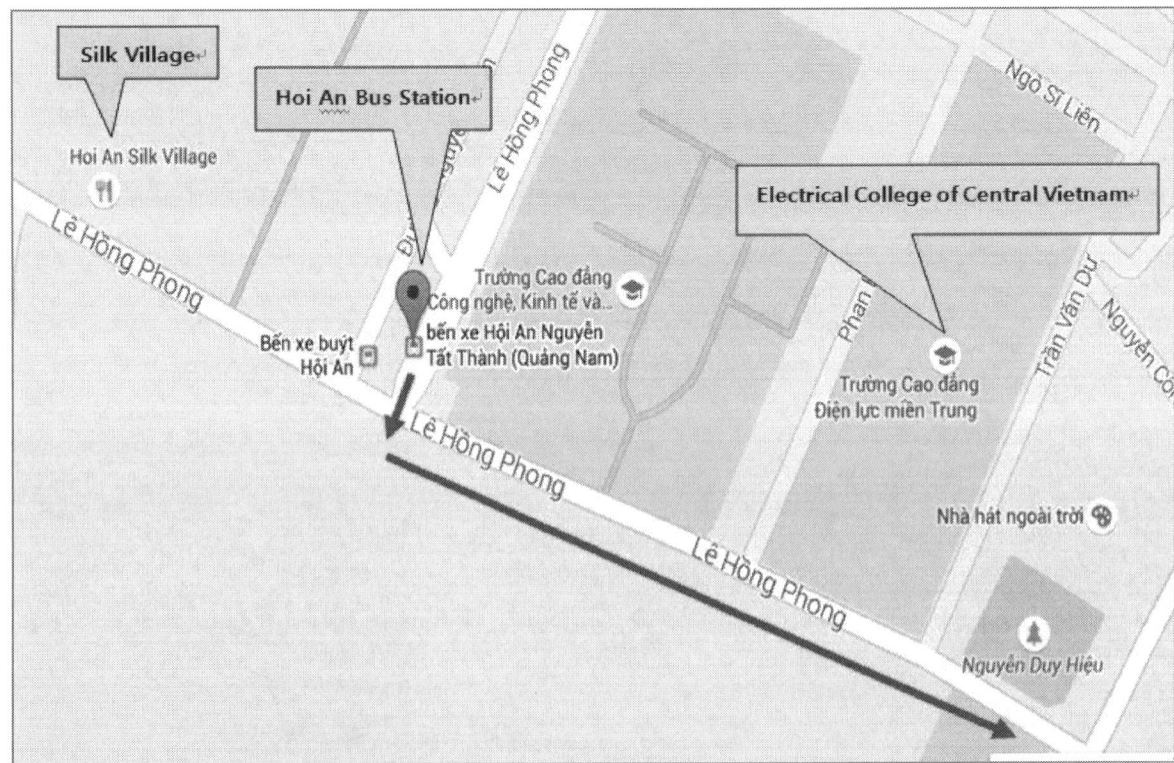

(When you come out of "Hoi An Bus Station", take the road towards "Electrical College of Central Vietnam". It's "Le Hong Phong Road". Do not take the road to "Silk Village" indicated on the left. The red arrows on the map show your way to "Old Town". Let's see the next map.)

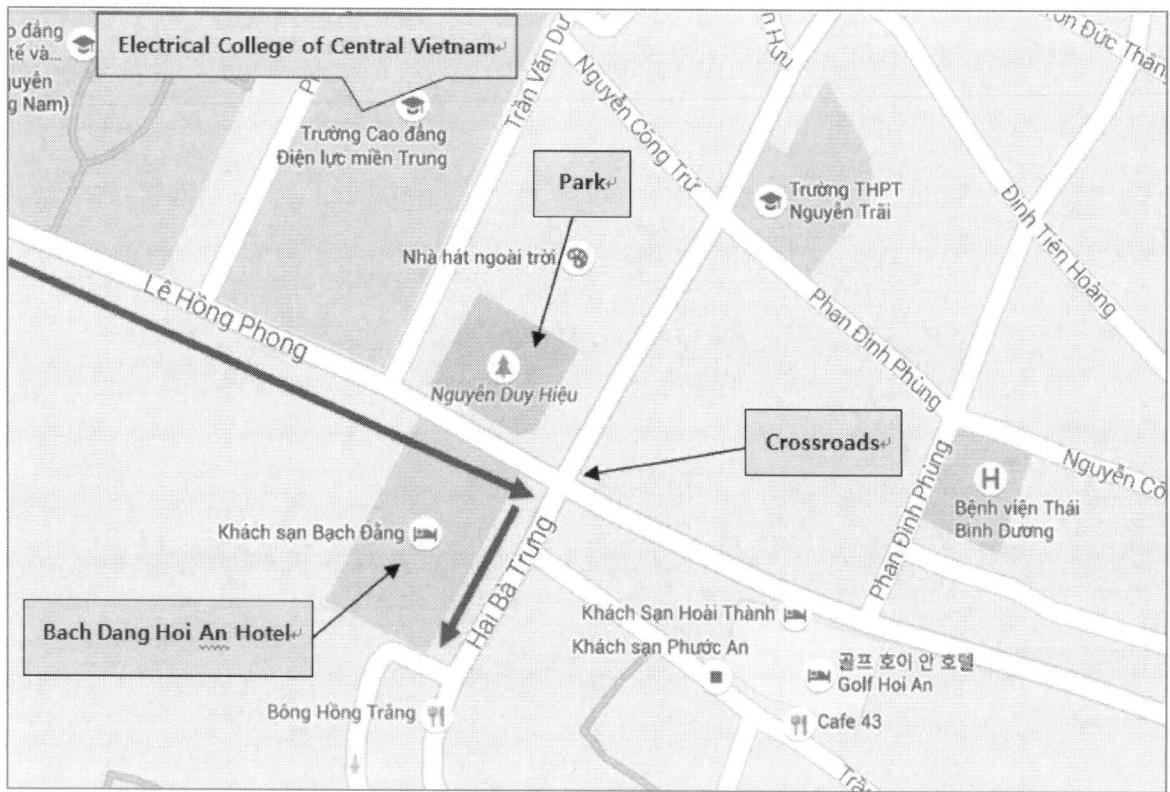

(After passing by "Electrical College of Central Vietnam", you will meet a crossroads shortly. A small park is on the left and "Bach Dang Hoi An Hotel" is on the right. Then, take the road of "Hai Ba Trung" as indicated by the second red arrow on the map. At the crossroads, you are going to the way to the right. Walk straight along the street of "Hai Ba Trung" and you will meet "Old Town" around in 10 minutes. Now, let's go from "Hoi An Bus Station" to "Old Town".)

(Hoi An Bus Station)

(Come out of the station as indicated by the yellow arrows on the photo. Go around 20 meters along the second arrow and you will meet a wide street of "Le Hong Phong". Then, turn to the left and you will find "Electrical College of Central Vietnam" on your left shortly.)

(A yellow arrow on the photo indicates your way to go.)

(Motorbikes are going to the street of "Le Hong Phong". Follow the yellow arrows to the left.)

(You are going to "Electrical College of Central Vietnam" along the road of "Le Hong Phong".)

(Le Hong Phong Road)

("Electrical College of Central Vietnam" on your left.)

("Le Hong Phong Road" after the college.)

("Bach Dang Hoi An Hotel" is standing on the other side of the road. A crossroads is ahead.)

("Bach Dang Hoi An Hotel")

(At this crossroads, go to the right. It's "Hai Ba Trung Road" towards "Old Town".)

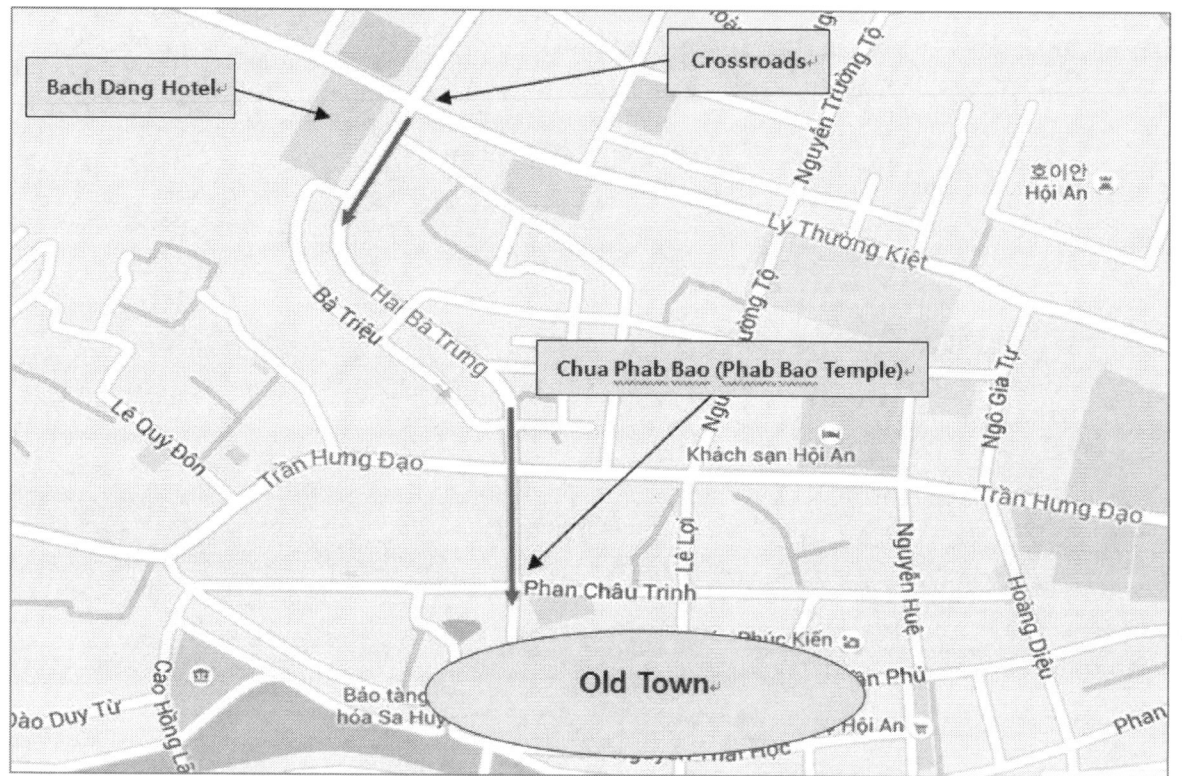

(Keep walking along the street of "Hai Ba Trung" like the first red arrow and you will meet "Chua Phab Bao", i.e. "Phab Bao Temple" in around 10 minutes. Go straight as the second arrow on the map and you will get "Old Town" shortly.

(The arrow on the photo indicates "Hai Ba Trung Road" at the junction. You will meet hotels, pubs, restaurants and travel agencies shortly. Keep walking along the road until Phab Bao Temple standing on the left.)

("Hai Ba Trung Road")

(Keep walking straight. Around 500 meters ahead, you will find the temple on the left.)

(You will meet "Chua Phab Bao", i.e. "Phab Bao Temple" at the end of this road.)

("Chua Phab Bao (Phab Bao Temple)")

(You are standing on the other side of the temple. Go straight along the road seen in front. Then, you will meet "Old Town" shortly.)

(After "Phab Bao Temple", you will go this narrow road. At the end of this road, "Old Town" begins. If you go to the right at the beginning of the town, you will meet "Cantonese Assembly Hall" and "Japanese Covered Bridge".)

("Old Town". You are looking at the road to the left.)

(You are looking right at the end of the narrow path. If you take this way, you will meet "Cantonese Assembly Hall" first. And, "Japanese Covered Bridge" will be followed. Here introduces the town on the right.)

("Cantonese Assembly Hall" is seen on the right. Another ticket you have to buy for admission.)

("Japanese Covered Bridge" is situated at the end of the road.)

(Entrance to "Japanese Covered Bridge".)

("Japanese Covered Bridge")

(A shrine in the middle of the bridge.)

(You are looking out from "Japanese Covered Bridge".)

("Old Town")

(Shops at "Old Town".)

(A cafe named "Ca Mai", i.e. "Mai Fish" on the right.)

("Mai Fish" is not old but new style.)

(An antique guest house.)

(She sells tasty bread on the street. After taking a stroll on the left road, go back to the right side of "Old Town". This is the end of your journey to "Da Nang" and "Old Town" at Hoi An. Now, let's go to "Ho Chi Minh City", the economic capital at the utmost southern part of Vietnam.)

Ho Chin Minh City

(Notre Dame Cathedral at Ho Chi Minh City.)

Content

1. City Summary

Ho Chi Minh City, formerly known as "Saigon", is worth to be called as the economic capital of Vietnam. Only Ho Chi Minh City in Vietnam is under construction of subway now.

For travelers, it's not difficult to take a look at the whole city on foot, because almost of all attractions are concentrated at city center. Hotels, restaurants and attractions are situated like a fan with Ho Chi Minh City Hall as their center. Even Reunification Palace, Notre Dame Cathedral and Central Post Office can be easily accessed from City Hall on foot. Opera House, another milestone of Ho Chi Minh City, is standing close to City Hall. You can also get Binh Tay Market, the biggest market of Ho Chi Minh City, by bus from Ben Thanh Bus Station, which is located only around 300 meters away from City Hall.

When you stand on a huge square in front of City Hall, you will meet a statue of Ho Chi Minh. He looks down on the vast square stretching out to Saigon River.

(You are looking at the heart of Ho Chi Minh City Center. Ho Chi Minh Statue is standing on the square. "City Hall" is standing behind the statue and Rex Hotel is situated on the left. The building on the right is a luxurious shopping mall of "Union Square".)

(1) Location

Ho Chi Minh City is located at the southern part of Vietnam.

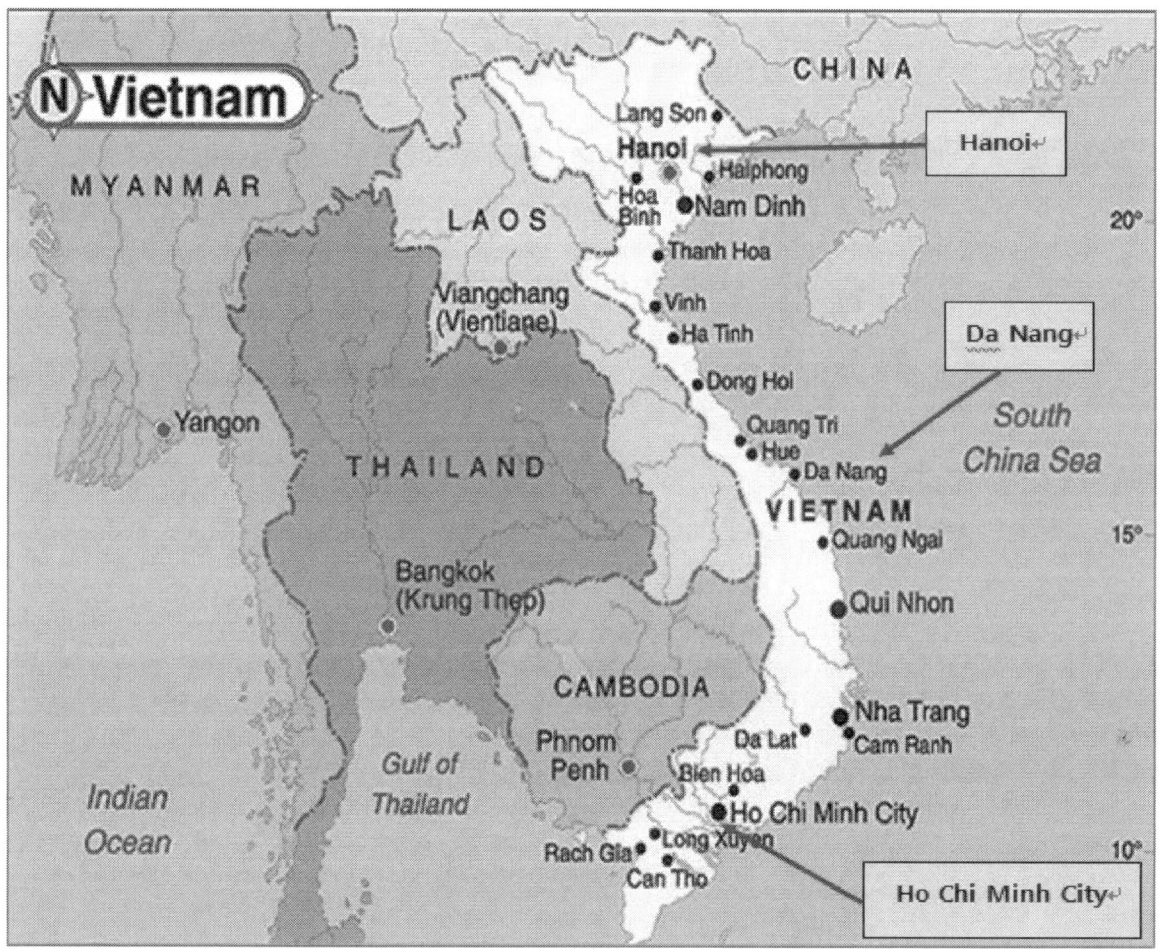

(Ho Chi Minh City, former "Saigon", is situated at the bottom of the long Vietnam. For the whole country, you can make an itinerary from Ho Chi Minh City to Hanoi via Da Nang and vise versa.)

(2) Currency

Vietnam Dong ("VND") is national currency of Vietnam. They simply say the price with the remains after cut off the last 3 digits on the currency. For example, they say only "500" in case of VND500,000. US$1.00 is around VND20,000 as of July 2015. In that case of VND20,000, you will hear "twenty".

(All monetary notes bear the portrait of Ho Chi Minh. They call the president as "Bac Ho" instead of "President Ho". "Bac Ho" means "Uncle Ho".)

(3) Language

Signs on the road and announcement on the bus are all stipulated only in Vietnamese language. On the other hand, signs at museums, menu at restaurants include French and English. Moreover, staff at hotel and tour guides speak English very well. Therefore, even a stranger at Ho Chi Minh City, you don't need to worry about the difficulty of language.

(Road names on the sign are all written only in Vietnamese language. Can you see the signboard hung on the building on the photo? There is no English on the board. Even bus stand and announcement on the bus are also served only in Vietnamese. However, airport, monuments, temples and restaurants have English signs and menu. Even you may feel a little confused in the beginning, you'll be accustomed shortly. It would be no matter for your wonderful journey at Ho Chi Minh City.)

(4) Heroes

There often appear 5 heroes in Vietnamese history. They are "Emperor Dinh Tien Hoang", "Emperor Ly Thai To", "General Tran Hung Dao", "General Le Loi (later "King Le Thai To") and "President Ho Chi Minh". You can find them on the name of many roads in Vietnam.

(a) Emperor Dinh Tien Hoang comes first in the order of history. He reunified the northern Vietnam for the first time in the 10th century.

(b) Next is Emperor Ly Thai To who moved the capital city of Vietnam from "Hoa Lu" to "Thang Long", current "Hanoi", in 1010.

(c) General Tran Hung Dao defeated Mongolian invasion in the 13th century. His shrine at Ho Chi Minh City will be introduced in detail later.

(d) General Le Loi (1385~1433) is a legendary hero who achieved Vietnamese Independence from China in the 15th century. Later his became King Le Thai To. One of the most important streets at Ho Chi Minh City is "Le Loi Road".

(e) Vietnamese people call Ho Chi Minh as "Bac Ho" rather than President Ho Chi Minh. "Bac Ho" means "Uncle Ho". If you pay a visit his humble one-story-house built on stilts in Hanoi where he lived since 1958 until his final day of the 2nd of September 1969, you will come know the reason why they love him so much. The Presidential Palace he refused to move in has still no owner yet.

(Ho Chi Minh Statue standing in front of City Hall.)

(5) City Center

As you see the map below, except the attractions around "Binh Tay Market" shown on the upper left, you can get nearly almost of all attractions on foot. Because, attractions are located like a fan with Ho Chi Minh City Hall (red mark on the map) as their center.

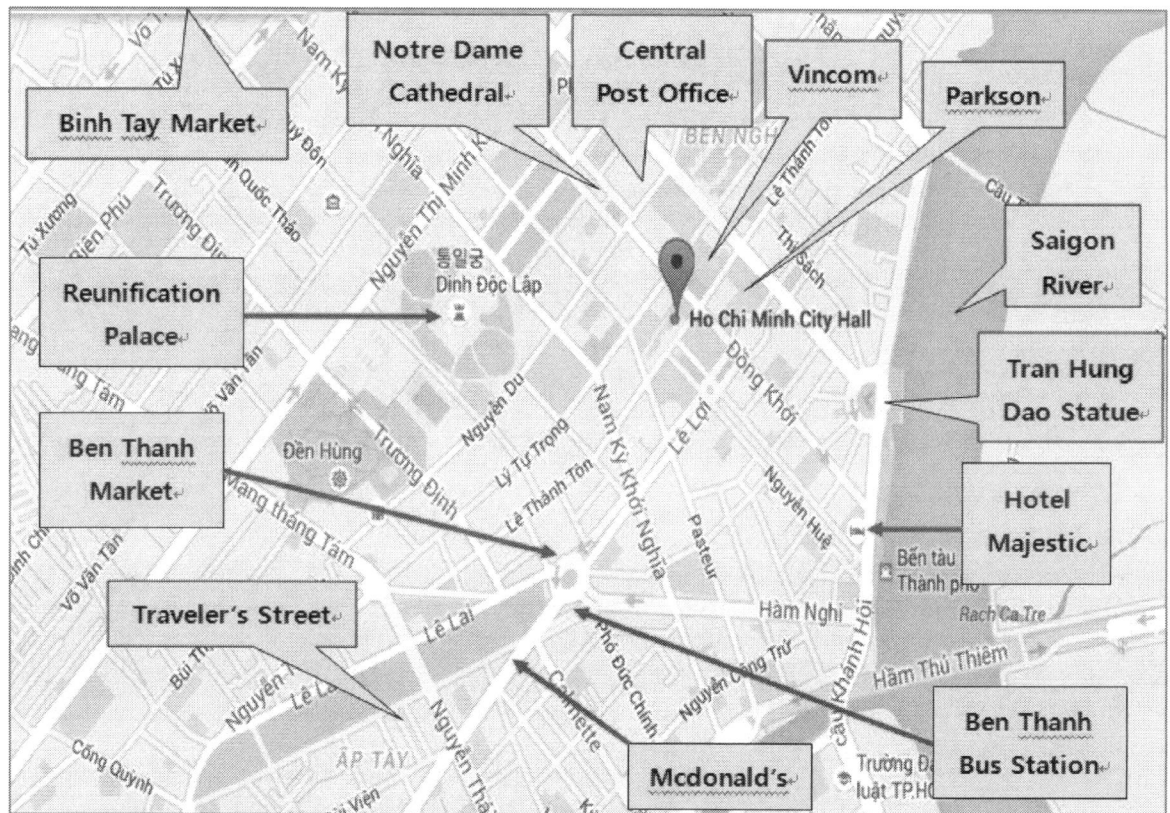

(When you go to the attractions around "Bin Tay Market", the biggest market in Ho Chi Minh City, take a bus No. 1 at "Ben Thanh Bus Station" which is indicated by a yellow box on the right bottom. Then, you will meet the market at its final stop.)

(From "Vincom", a fantastic shopping mall with a food court and a supermarket, you are looking down on the heart of HO Chi Minh City. A huge square will be unveiled in front of "City Hall". A statue of Ho Chi Minh is standing in a small park at the beginning of the square. Rex Hotel and Union Square are surrounding the statue. The name of the street between City Hall and Union Square is "Le Thanh Ton".

There are 2 more important streets to remember for the attractions at the city center. They are "Dong Koi Road" and "Hai Ba Trung Road". If you follow the street of "Dong Koi", you will meet "Opera House", "Union Square", "Parkson Mall", "Vincom" and even "Notre Dame Cathedral". When you walk the street of "Hai Ba Trung" which is next to "Dong Koi Road", you will meet "Tran Hung Dao Statue" standing near the Saigon River. "Hai Long 5 Hotel", a cheap and clean hotel at the city center, which will be introduced in detail at "4. Hotels", is located at the street, too.)

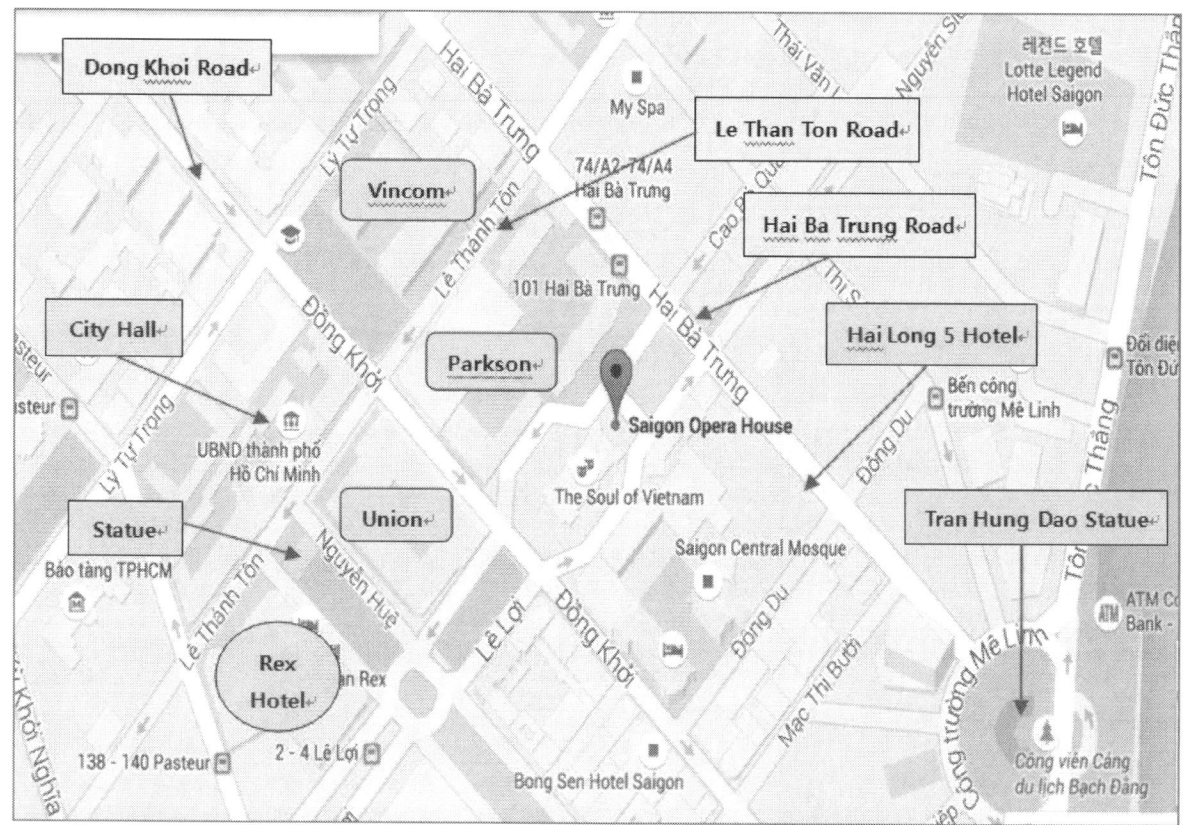

("Saigon Opera House", indicated by a red mark on the map, is situated between "Dong Koi Road" and "Ha Ba Trung Road". City Hall, Union Square and Rex Hotel are located on "Le Than Ton Road". And, many other attractions are also disposed on the 3 streets.)

("Opera House" at "Dong Koi Road".)

2. Public Transportation

They prepare signs on the road very well. Therefore, if you have address, you can find them with ease. Subway is under construction. However, there are so many buses even no English. A little difficult in Vietnamese language, you can find fun when you try a bus No. 01 in case of attractions around "Binh Tay Market" at China Town. And, No. 152 will take you to "Tan Son Nhat International Airport" of Ho Chi Minh City.

When you try bus, search the official site first and make sure through inquiry to front desk of your hotel. They will give you information about where to take the bus. Let's take a look at the site below.

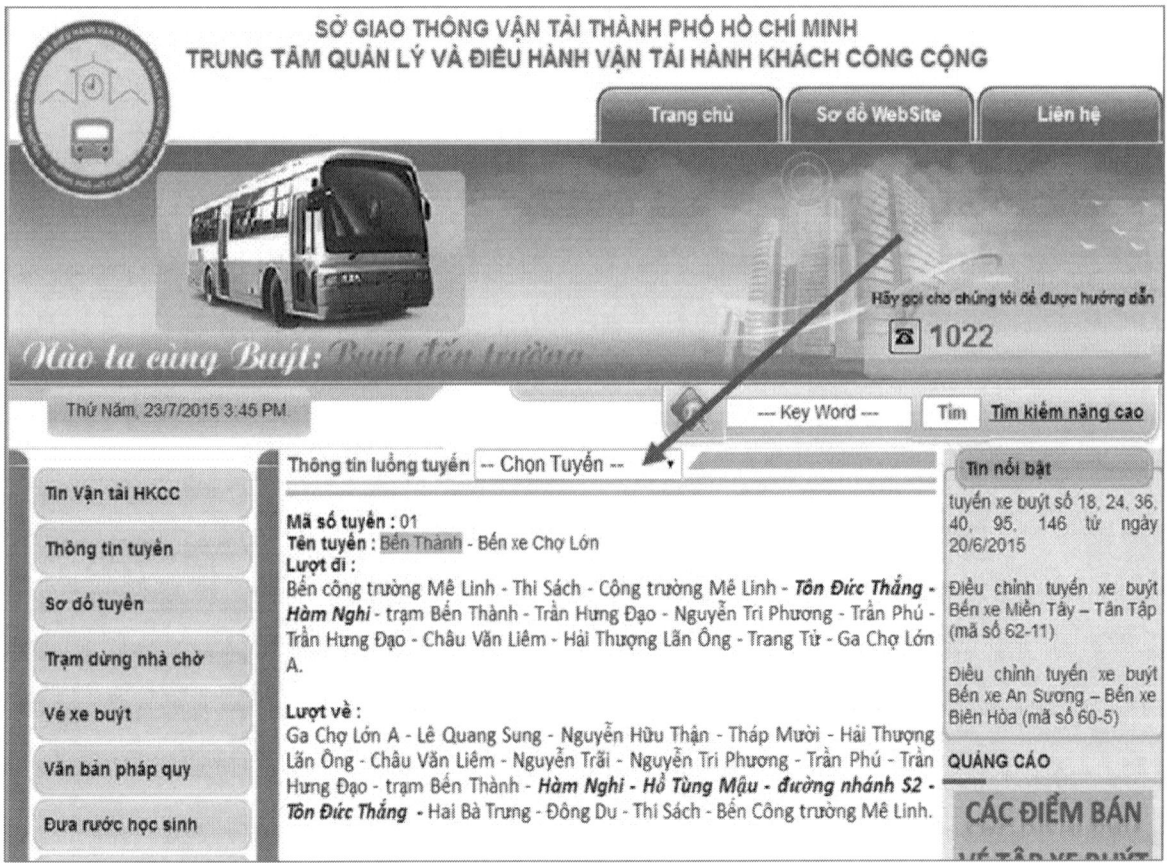

http://www.buyttphcm.com.vn/Detail_TTLT.aspx?sl=01

When you click the URL, you will meet this screen first. Then, use the search column indicated by the red arrow on the photo. Even stated only in Vietnamese, you can catch the meaning. "Ben Xe" means "Bus". Next photo shows you an example.)

322

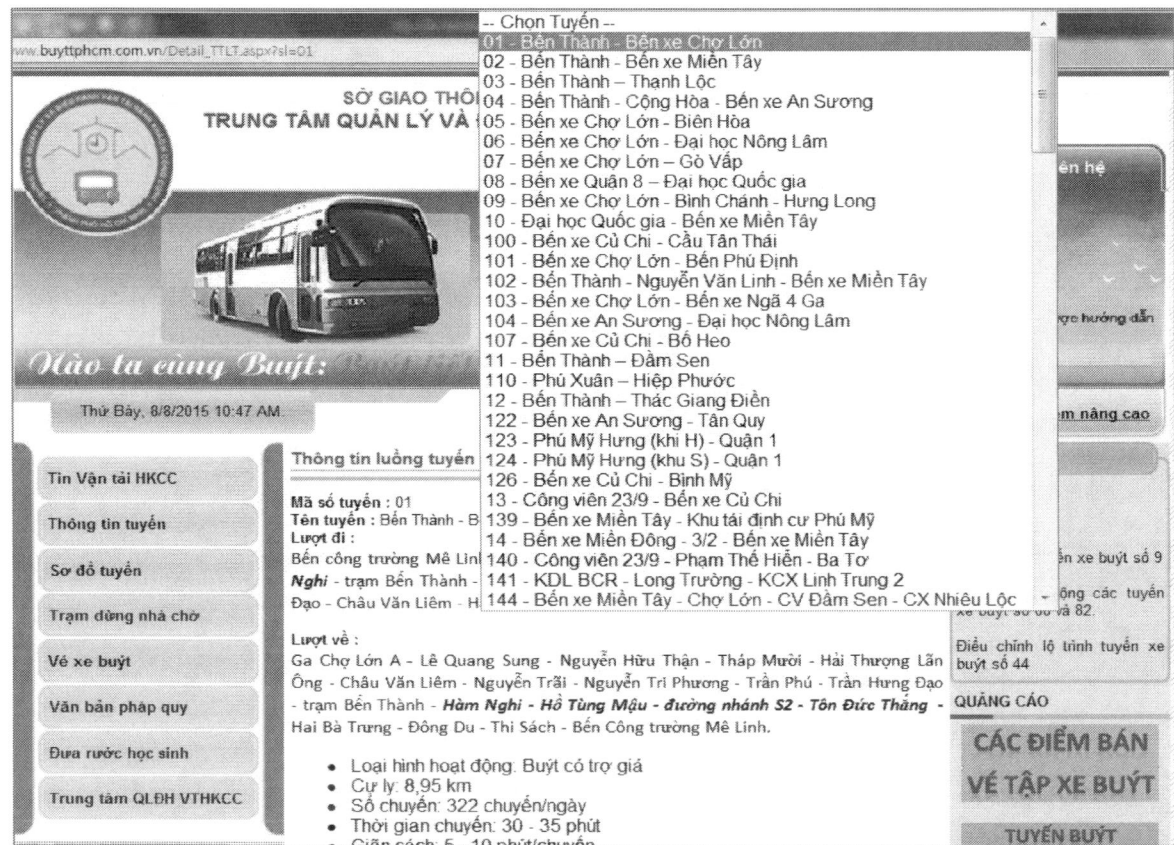

When you go to "Binh Tay Market", you will have the information that the market is near "Cho Lon Bus Station". If you have a lodge at city center, your close bus terminal must be "Ben Thanh Bus Station", which is located on the opposite side of the famous market of "Ben Thanh". When you click the search column, they will show you list of buses. For the bus from "Ben Thanh Bus Station" to "Cho Lon Bus Station" is shown at the first row. Choose the first row and they will show you bus numbers, kilometers and time to be taken. In this case, you will take a bus No. 01 at "Ben Thanh Bus Station" bound for "Cho Lon Bus Station".

If you walk from "Opera House" at city center to "Ben Thanh Bus Station", it takes around 15 minutes. However, there are many buses going to the bus terminal. Ask your front desk and they will tell you where you can take a bus towards "Ben Thanh Bus Station".)

(A bus stand on the street of "Hai Ba Trung".)

(A bus No. 03 bound for "Ben Thanh Bus Station" is waiting for passengers on "Hai Ba Trung Road". Now, let's take a look at "Ben Thanh Bus Station" and "Cho Lon Bus Station" next.)

(1) Ben Thanh Bus Station (Bến xe Bến Thành)

When you travel at city center, "Ben Thanh Bus Station" is the most convenient bus terminal. It is located on the opposite side of the famous market of "Ben Thanh". It takes around 15 minutes from city center on foot. And, you can also take buses to the terminal. Many buses running on the road of "Dong Koi" and "Hai Ba Trung" bound for the bus station.

For the attractions around "Binh Tay Market" at China Town, you will take a bus No. 01 at the bus station. It takes around 30 minutes and costs VND5,000.

For "Tan Son Nhat International Airport", take a bus No. 152 at "Ben Thanh Bus Station". It costs VND5,000 plus extra VND5,000 in case of big luggage. You will arrive at the airport in around 30 minutes.

When you come from city center by bus, you may take No. 03, 19 or 26 on the street of "Hai Ba Trung". It costs VND6,000.

(On a huge rotary, "Ben Thanh Bus Station" and "Ben Thanh Market" are facing each other. If you follow the road by the park, you will meet "De Tham Road", a Travelers' Sreet, in 20 minutes.)

("Ben Thanh Bus Station". There are 4 lanes with the information sign on each head.)

(Ben Thanh Bus Station. You can see the wide red sign in a distance.)

(Ben Thanh Bus Station. Place for bus arrival is behind the lanes for boarding.)

(Bus No. 152 for "Tan Song Nhat International Airport". To "Cho Lon Bus Station" for "Binh Tay Market" in China Town, take a bus No. 01.)

(When you arrive at "Ben Thanh Bus Station", you will find a Mcdonald's (photo) standing on the opposite side of the road. It is located by the park towards "De Tham Road", a travelers' street. You may take a rest at the cool fast food store.)

(2) Cho Lon Bus Station (Bến xe Chợ Lớn)

Except the attractions around "Binh Tay Market" at China Town, you can get all attractions at Ho Chi Minh City on foot. For the attractions at China Town, you have to take a bus No. 01 at "Ben Thanh Bus Station" bound for "Cho Lon Bus Station". It takes around 30 minutes and costs VND5,000.

There are 3 attractions recommendable at China Town. They are "Binh Tay Market", the biggest one of Ho Chi Minh City, and "Cha Tam Church (Nha Tho Cha Tam)" together with a Chinese shrine of "Ong Bon Pagoda (二 府 廟 Mieu Nhi Phu)". You can get them all in around 15 minutes on foot from "Cho Lon Bus Station".

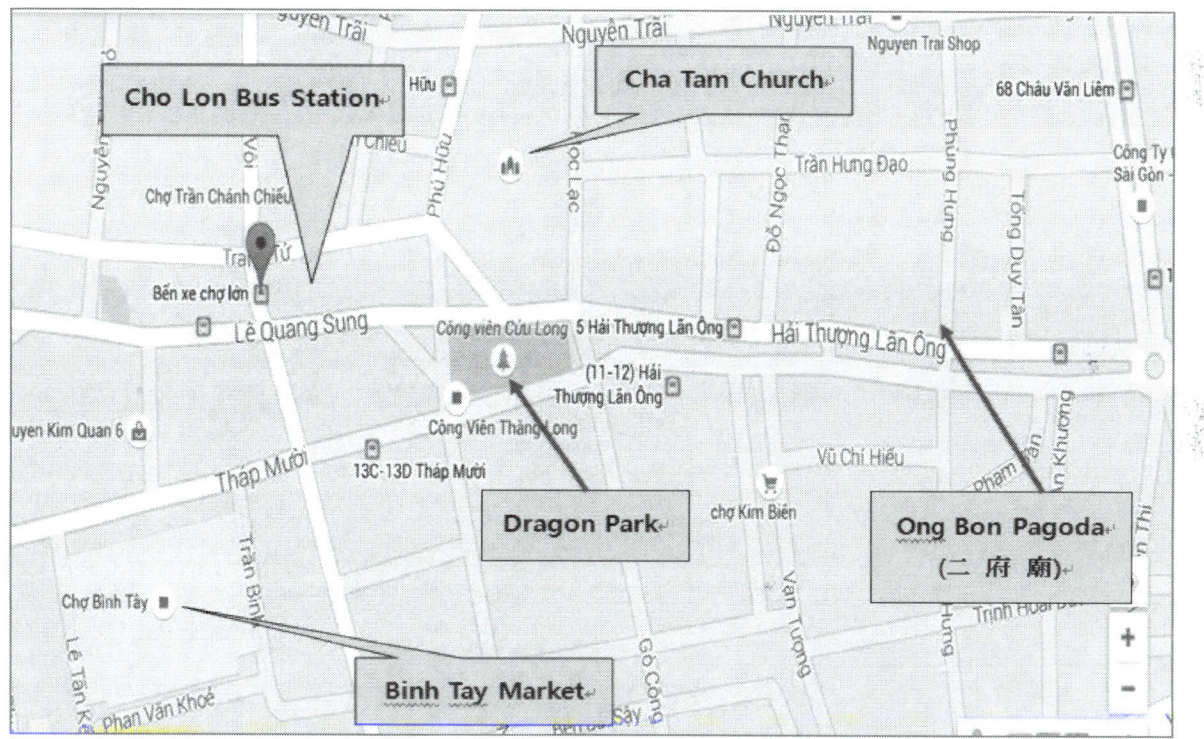

(When you arrive at "Cho Lon Bus Station", look back and you will find a soaring spire behind the bus terminal. It's "Cha Tam Church". After the church, take the wide road of "Hai Thuong Lan Ong" and you will meet a Chinese temple of "Ong Bon Pagoda (二 府 廟 Mieu Nhi Phu)" in 10 minutes. "Binh Tay Market" is located around 10-minute-walk away from "Cho Lon Bus Station".)

(Bus No. 01 bound for "Cho Lon Bus Station". Cool and clean.)

(Cho Lon Bus Station. Buses are coming into the terminal through this gate. When you get off the bus, look behind. And, you will find "Cha Tam Church" standing high.)

(You are looking back at "Cha Tam Church".)

(Why don't you take a look at the street market just in front of the arrival gate of "Cho Lon Bus Station"?)

("Cha Tam Church (Nha Tho Cha Tam. 方濟各天主堂)". It takes not more than 10 minutes from "Cho Lon Bus Station" on foot.)

(A small park with a dragon in the pond. 5 minutes from "Cho Lon Bus Station" on foot.)

("Ong Bon Pagoda (二府廟. Mieu Nhi Phu)". It takes 10 minutes on foot from "Cha Tam Church".)

("Binh Tay Market". Only 10 minutes on foot from "Cho Lon Bus Station".)

3. Hotel

Many travelers make reservation for a hotel at "De Tham Road". The travelers' street has many cheap hotels, pubs, restaurants and travel agencies. However, it is located a little far from city center. It takes around 20 minutes on foot from city center.

On the other hand, there also are many cheap and clean hotels at city center where luxurious hotels are crowded in such as Rex, Majestic, Continental, Park Hyatt, Caravelle and Sheraton Hotel. In consideration of many attractions and restaurants at the city center, a budget hotel near "Opera House", a milestone of city center, is strongly recommended to be booked.

Here introduces "Hai Long 5 Hotel" standing on "Hai Ba Trung Road" at city center. It is located around 5-minute-walk away from "Opera House". Except its convenient location, their morning buffet is fantastic. When you check-in, you have to deposit your passport to the front in Vietnam. Therefore, when you are going to change money at a bank, you have to take the passport back from the front desk. Banks require your passport when exchange money.

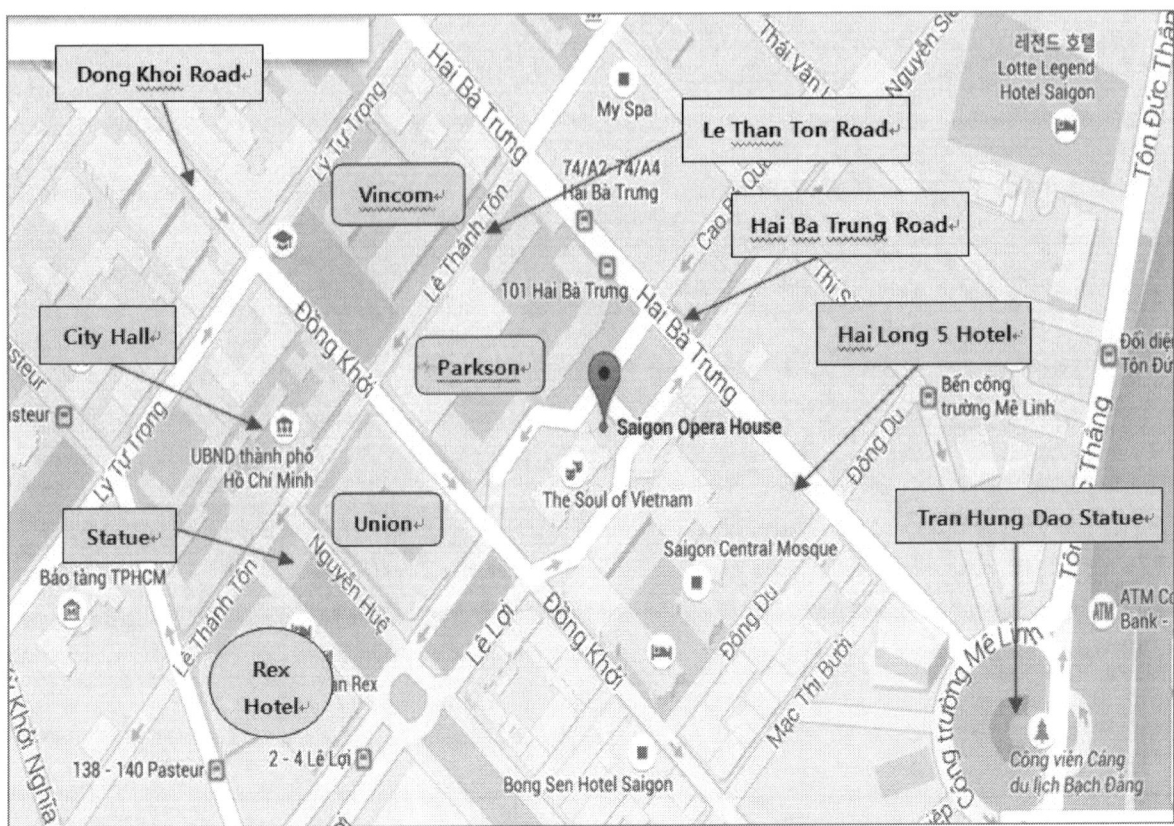

(You will meet the tasty food courts at "Vincom Center" and "Parkson". "Tran Hung Dao Statue" standing near the "Saigon River", is 5-minute-walk away from "Hai Long 5 Hotel".)

("Hai Long 5 Hotel" is standing on the street of "Hai Ba Trung", where motorbikes are running on.)

(A car is parking in front of "Hai Long 5 Hotel". A Starbucks Coffee and a supermarket of "Green Gourmet Market" are situated just 50 meters away from the hotel.)

(Entrance to "Ha Long 5 Hotel".)

(A buffet restaurant prepared for breakfast. They serve from 06:30 until 09:30 in the morning. Baguette, yogurt, congee, vegetables, meats and fresh fruits are all fantastic.)

4. Attractions

Ho Chi Minh City, formerly known as "Saigon", is the economic capital of Vietnam. Almost of all attractions at this big city, are all crowded at the city center. City center consists of (1) hot places such as City Hall, Opera House, Mariamman Hindu Temple, Notre Dame Cathedral, Reunification Palace and Central Post Office, (2) luxurious hotels of Rex, Majestic, Continental, Park Hyatt, Sheraton and Caravelle, (3) shopping malls such as Union Square, Louis Vuitton, Vincom Center and Parkson, (4) Bin Thanh Market and Bin Thanh Bus Station for China Town and airport.

If you walk around 20 minutes from city center, you can get (5) Le Van Tam Park & Tran Hung Dao Temple dedicated to the general who defeated the Mongolian invasion in the 13th century. You can also get (6) the travelers' street on "De Tham Road" in 20-minute-walk from the center. If you remember the 3 key roads at the city center, it's very helpful to get the attractions. They are "Dong Khoi", "Hai Ba Trung" and "Le Loi Road" indicated by the pink boxes on the map below.

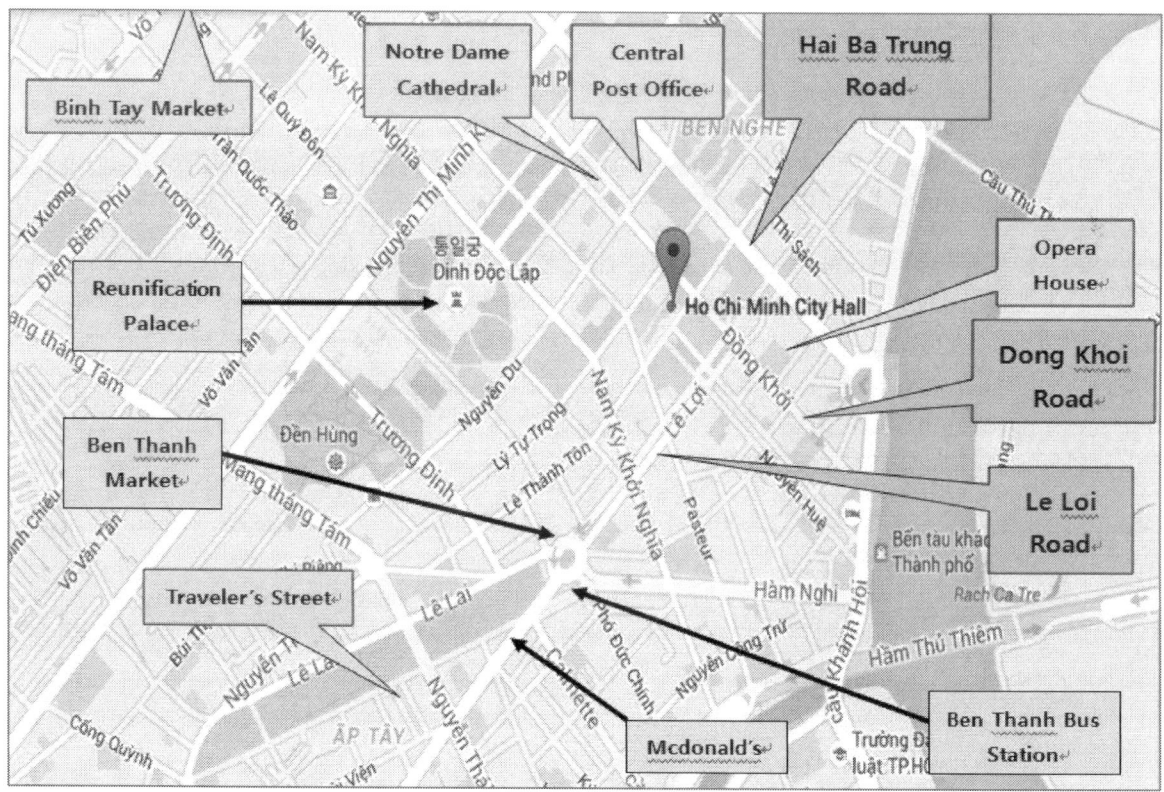

("Opera House" is standing on "Dong Khoi Road" and "Hai Long 5 Hotel" is situated near the Municipal Theater. Reunification Palace and Notre Dame Cathedral are 20-minute-walk away from Opera House.)

This book will introduces the attractions in the order stated as below. The 12 hot places will be approached from "Hai Long 5 Hotel", which is standing on the street of "Hai Ba Trung" at city center.

(1) Ho Chi Minh City Hall

(2) Opera House

(3) Notre Dame Cathedral

(4) Central Post Office

(5) Reunification Palace

(6) Ben Thanh Market

(7) Fine Arts Museum

(8) De Tham Road (Travelers' Street)

(9) Mariamman Hindu Temple

(10) Saigon Riverside

(11) China Town (Binh Tay Market, Cha Tam Church, Ong Bon Pagoda (二府廟))

(12) Le Van Tam Park & Tran Hung Dao Temple

Here shows you an enlarged map below for the heart of city center.

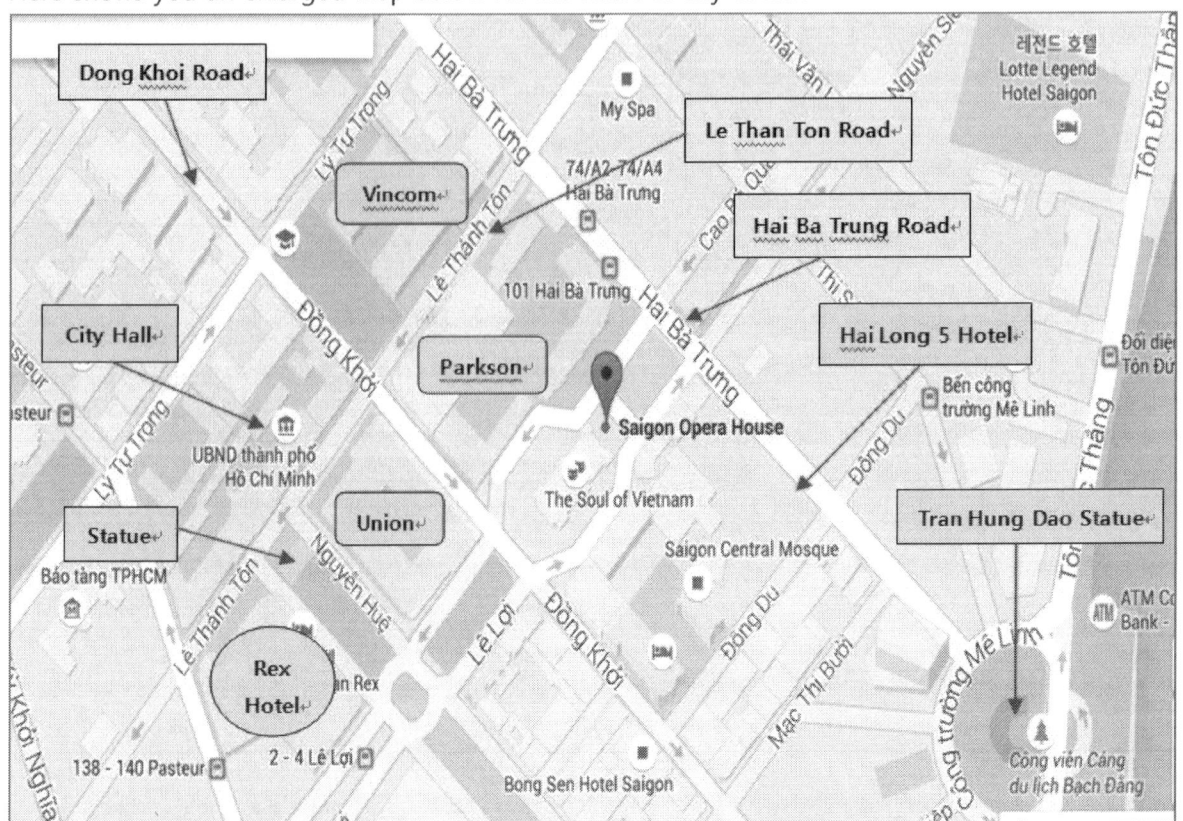

(Try the food courts at Vincom Center and Parkson. They are tasty at reasonable price.)

(A sign near "Vincom Center" standing at "Dong Khoi Road".)

(1) Ho Chi Minh City Hall

City Hall, i.e. "People's Committee Head Office", has been completed after for 6-year-construction since 1902. It's the most graceful French-style building at Ho Chi Minh City and beloved as the icon of the city. No entrance but you can take photos of the beautiful house.

There is a huge square in front of City Hall with a statue of Ho Chi Minh at the beginning. It's a long and wide square stretching from the hall until to the Saigon River. The luxurious Rex Hotel and a gorgeous shopping mall of "Union Square" are standing on each side of the statue.

Different from the luxurious shopping mall of "Louis Vuitton" standing near "Opera House", "Vincom Center" and "Parkson" situated near City Hall are very helpful for budget travelers to Ho Chi Minh City. They have shopping malls, supermarkets and food courts. After Ho Chi Minh City Hall, the 2 malls will be introduced in detail.

(You are standing at the square and looking at Ho Chi Minh City Hall. A statue is standing in front of the hall. Rex Hotel is on the left and Union Square is on the right. When you approach the statue too closely, the guards at the square will stop you.

Ho Chi Minh refused to move in Presidential Palace and lived in a humble house-on-stilts at Hanoi until he died. Vietnamese respect Ho Chi Minh so much that they call him "Bac Ho", i.e. "Uncle Ho" rather than "President Ho".)

NGUYỄN ÁI QUỐC. NĂM 1924.
Nguyen Ai Quoc en 1924.
Nguyen Ai Quoc in 1924.

(Ho Chi Minh was called as "Nguyen Ai Quoc" in his youth. This photo was taken in 1924 when he was 34 years old. Good looking.)

(Way to Ho Chi Minh City Hall.)

City Hall is situated around 5-minute-walk away from "Opera House" and 10 minutes from "Hai Long 5 Hotel" on the street of "Hai Ba Trung". Vincom Center and Parkson are also located near City Hall.

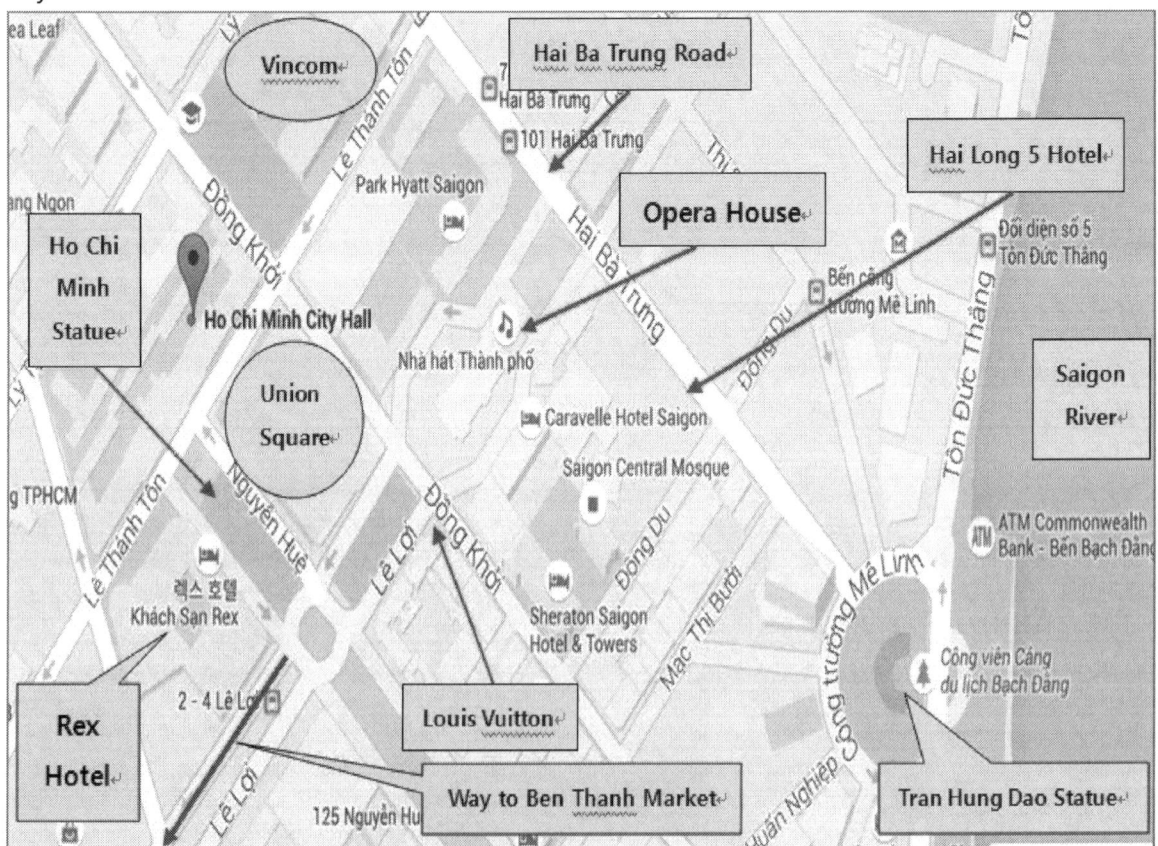

(In case from "Hai Long 5 Hotel", go along the street of "Hai Ba Trung" until "Vincom Center" and turn left at the end of Park Hyatt Saigon. Go straight along the road of "Le Thanh Ton" with "Vincom Centre" on your right and "Parkson" on your left. At a junction crossed with "Dong Khoi Road", you will find Union Square on your left. Ho Chi Minh City Hall is standing on the opposite side of the mall. An enlarged map for the way to City Hall will be suggested next.

In case from "Opera House", go along the street of "Dong Khoi" until the junction crossed with "Le Thanh Ton Road" and you will find Union Square on your left. Ho Chi Minh City Hall is standing on the other side of the road of Le Than Ton.

As explained earlier, Rex Hotel and Union Square are situated on both sides of City Hall. A subway construction is under way near Rex Hotel. Therefore, "Le Loi Road", the way from Rex Hotel to "Ben Thanh Market" and "Ben Thanh Bus Station", is nearly blocked by fence. However, you can get the market and bus terminal through a narrow path prepared in front of the hotel.)

(From "Vincom Center, you are looking down on "Le Thanh Ton Road", where City Hall and Union Square are facing each other.)

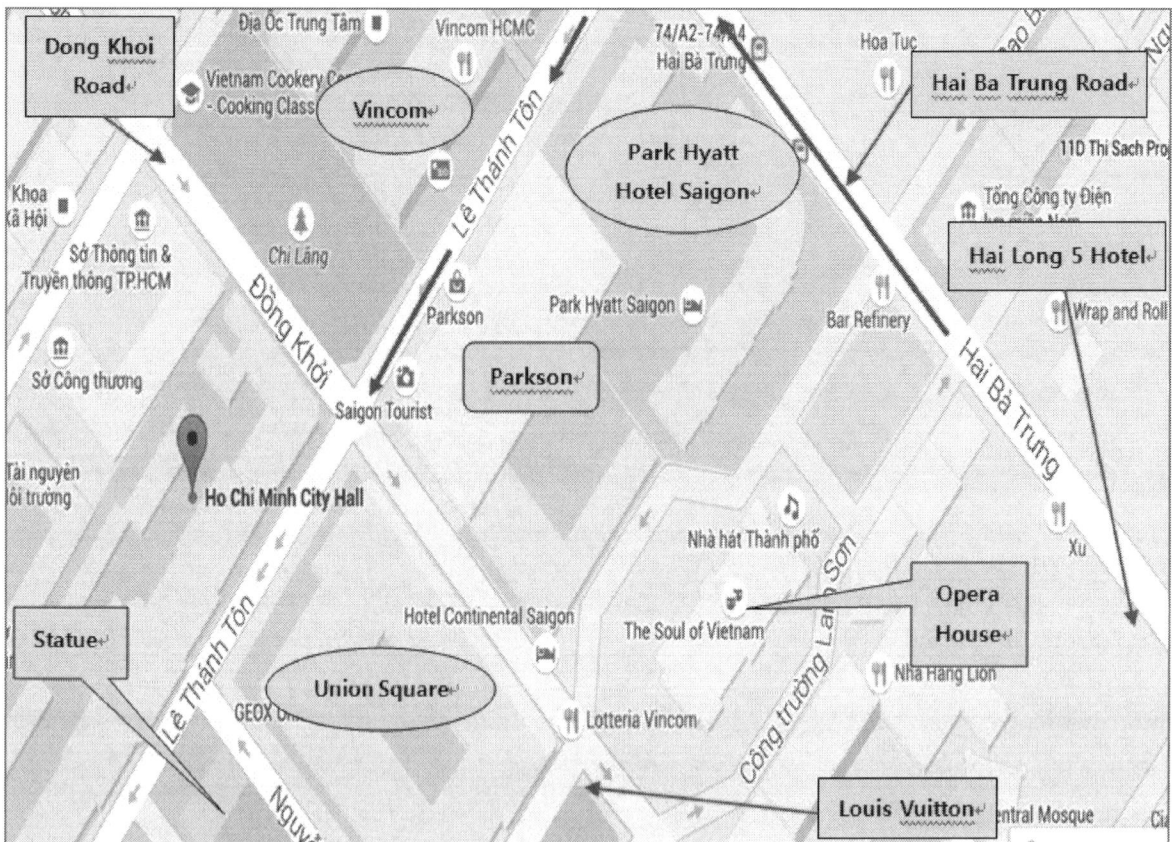

(An enlarged map from "Hai Long 5 Hotel" to City Hall.

When you start from "Hai Long 5 Hotel", follow the first red arrow indicated on "Hai Ba Trung" Road" and turn left to the street of "Le Thanh Ton" as the second arrow on the map. Go straight as the third arrow with "Vincom Center" on your right and "Parkson" on your left. Then, you will meet a junction shortly. At the junction crossed with "Dong Khoi Road", you will find "Saigon Tourist" on your left. Cross the road straight and you will find City Hall on your right.

In case from Opera House, only go one block along "Dong Khoi Road" and you will meet Union Square on your left. City Hall is standing on the opposite side of the mall.

Now, let's go to Ho Chi Minh City Hall along the street of "Hai Ba Trung".)

(From "Hai Long 5 Hotel", you are walking on the street of "Hai Ba Trung". Pass through "Park Hyatt Hotel" seen on the photo and follow the yellow arrow on the photo until the end of this hotel.)

(From Park Hyatt Hotel, you are looking at restaurant "Argentina" (left) and pub "Beirut" (right) on the other side of "Hai Ba Trung Road".)

(At the end of Park Hyatt Hotel, you are looking back at "Hai Ba Trung Road". A tall building standing on the right is "Vietcom Ban Tower" near the Saigon River. "Hai Long 5 Hotel" is located between Park Hyatt Hotel and Vietcom Bank Tower.)

(You've already turned to the left and are walking to "Parkson" along the road of "Le Thanh Ton". Vincom Center is standing on the right. You will meet a junction crossed with "Dong Khoi Road" shortly. Then, cross the junction straight and you will meet Union Square on your left and City Hall on your right.)

(You are looking at "Vincom Center" from "Parkson". It has shopping malls, a supermarket and a food court.)

(On the contrary, you are looking at Parkson this time from Vincom Center. It also has malls, a supermarket and a food court.)

(After crossing the junction straight, you are looking back at "Saigon Tourist" at the crossroads. "Vincom Center" is standing on the left and "Parkson" is hidden behind "Saigon Tourist".)

(Just after the junction, you are looking back at Vincom Center.)

(You will see Ho Chi Minh City Hall just after the junction. Union Square is partly seen on the far left side on the photo.)

(City Hall at night.)

(Union Square. You will meet this mall on your left just after the junction. City Hall is standing on the right.)

(Union Square, a luxurious shopping mall, at night)

(Ho Chi Minh Statue is standing in front of City Hall.)

(You are looking at City Hall from the vast people's square. Rex Hotel is standing on the left and Union Square is on the right.)

(City Hall from people's square at night.)

(People are enjoying the fountain on the square.)

(You are looking at Rex Hotel. The street of "Le Loi" in front of the hotel has been blocked by a fence due to construction of subway. However, they prepared a narrow path just in front of the hotel for "Ben Thanh Market" and "Ben Thanh Bus Station".)

(Shop "Chanel" occupies the ground floor of Rex Hotel. You can find a narrow path to "Ben Thanh Market" prepared beside the shop.)

(You are looking at the square with your back to Ho Chi Minh City Hall. It goes long until the Saigon River. The tallest building standing on the right is "Bitexco Financial Tower". It has an observatory at the 49th floor. VND200,000. www.sigonskydeck.com)

(From the same place at night. Now, let's take a look at Vincom Center and Parkson one by one.)

(Vincom Center)

Vincom Center is a skyscraper standing between "Hai Ba Trung Road" and "Dong Khoi Road". It consists of 2 blue buildings. You can find it in a distance.

(From "Dong Khoi Road", you look at Vincom Center. Parkson is partly seen behind the center.)

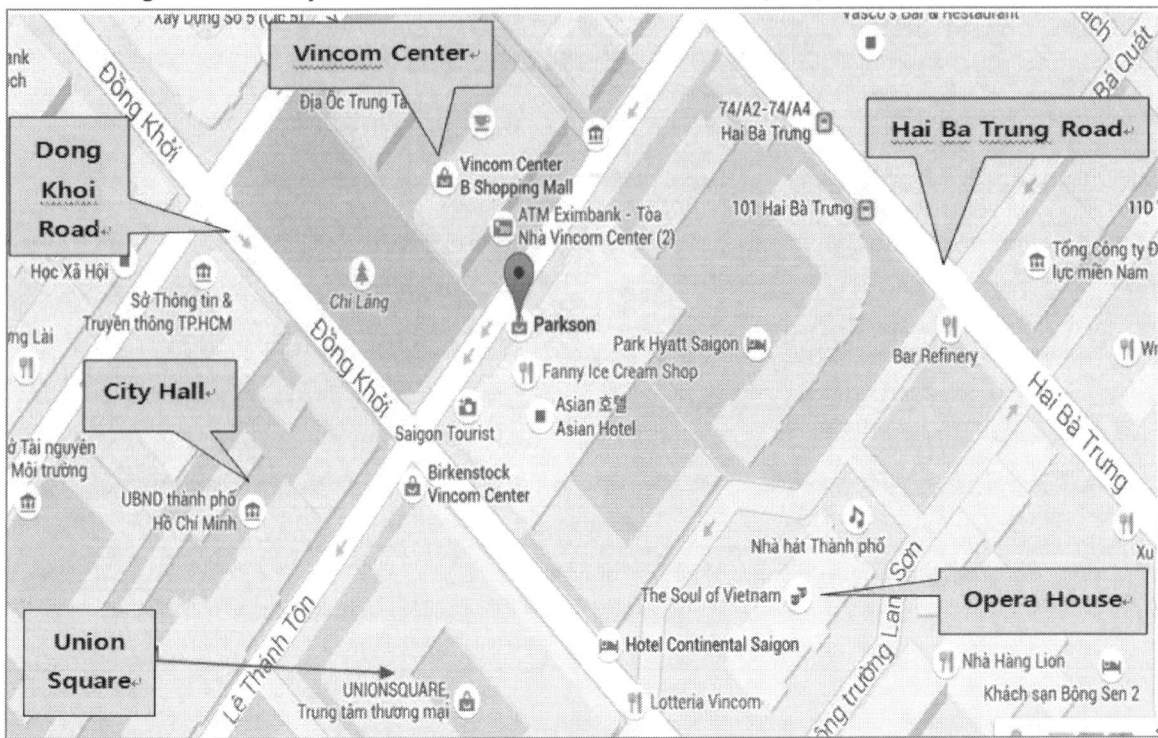

(Vincom Center and Parkson are facing each other on the street of "Le Thanh Ton".)

(Vincom Center)

(Vincom Center at night.)

(Inside Vincom Center.)

(You are looking down on a cafe on the ground floor.)

(A delicious bakery "Tous Les Jours".)

(Food center)

("Highlands Coffee")

(Supermarket "Vinmart")

(Parkson)

Parkson is located on the opposite side of Vincom Center. The food court on the 4ᵗʰ level of Parkson is strongly recommended for budget travelers. You can taste many kinds of food from the world at cheap price.

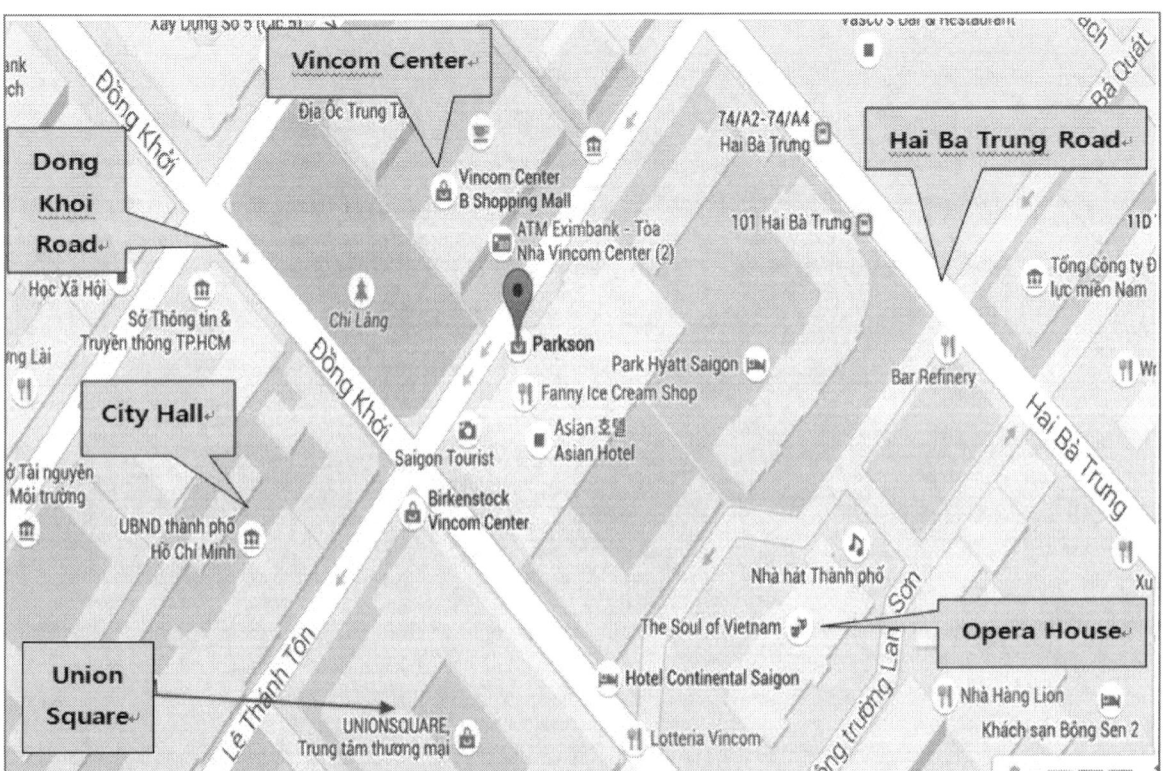

(Parkson (red mark on the map) is situated on the opposite side of Vincom Center. "Saigon Tourist" and Hotel Continental Saigon are near Parkson. Hotel Park Hyatt Saigon is situated behind Parkson.)

(From Vincom Center, you are looking at Parkson on the street of "Le Thanh Ton".)

(Face of Parkson on the street of "Dong Khoi". Hotel Continental Saigon (white) is next to Parkson to the right. Hotel Caravelle is standing high behind Continental.)

("Saigon Tourist" is standing on the far left. To the right, Ash Hotel, Parkson and Hotel Continental Saigon (white).)

(Citimart (Aeon) at the 4th floor of Parkson.)

(Food Court by Citimart. Cheap and delicious foods from the world. Highlands Coffee and fast food stores such as KFC and Lotteria are packed at the food court.)

(2) Opera House (Municipal Theatre)

Opera House with 1,800 seats was constructed in 1900 and has been completely remodeled through a renovation in 1998. Except random classic performance, the municipal theater is not open to the public. However, you can take photos of the gorgeous French-style house. It takes only 5 minutes on foot to Ho Chi Minh City Hall.

Not only City Hall but so many attractions, luxurious hotels, pubs and restaurants are near Opera House. They are Louis Vuitton, Union Square, Parkson, Hotel Continental Saigon, Park Hyatt Hotel, Vincom Center, Highlands Coffee, Hotel Caravelle, Chinese restaurant "泓 龍 軒 (Dragon Restaurant)", Pub "Lion", Korean Restaurant "Arirang" and 3 shops selling beautiful replica of sailboat standing on the street.

(Opera House. A just married couple are taking photos in front of the municipal theater.)

(Opera House and surroundings)

If you go to Opera House from "Hai Long 5 Hotel" on "Hai Ba Trung Road", it takes only around 5 minutes on foot.

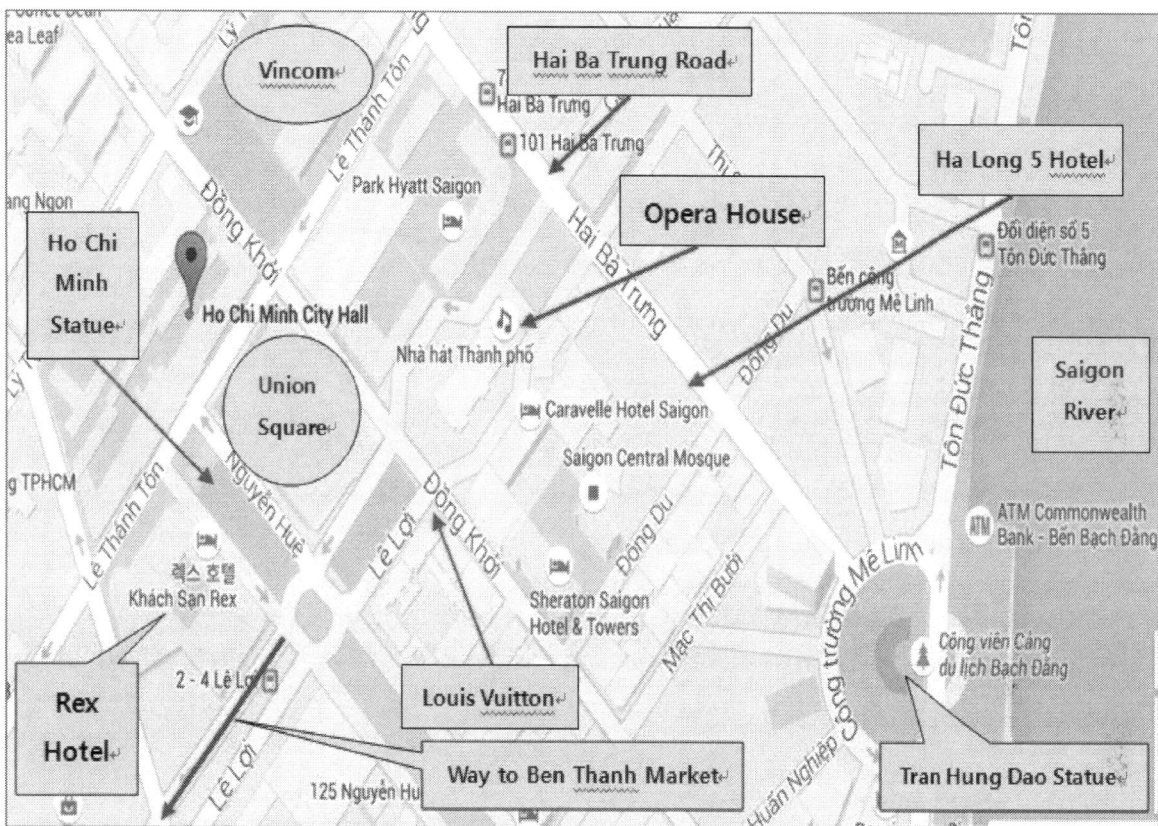

(When you stand in front of Opera House, you will find a Louis Vuitton shop standing on the opposite corner. Hotel Continental Saigon is located just on the right and Union Square is sitting on the other side of "Dong Khoi Road", which is lying in front of Opera House. Parkson (mall) is standing next to Hotel Continental Saigon.)

(Opera House. It is standing on the street of "Dong Khoi". Hotel Continental Saigon is on the left and Park Hyatt Hotel is behind the hotel. Hotel Caravelle is standing high on the far right on the photo. Stand in front of the house with your back to the entrance and you will find a Louis Vuitton shop on the left opposite corner of the road.)

(Opera House. A new married couple is taking photos. Hotel Caravelle Saigon is standing in front.)

(From the entrance to Opera House, you are looking left opposite. A Louis Vuitton shop is standing on the opposite corner. Hotel Carvelle is standing far left.)

(You are looking right from Opera House. 2 blue buildings of Vincom Center are standing tall behind Hotel Continental Saigon of 4 storied building seen in front. Parkson (mall) is situated next to the hotel on the street of "Dong Khoi", where motorbikes are running on. From the hotel, Union Square is located on the other side of the road. Park Hyatt Hotel is situated behind Continental Hotel.)

(Opera House (far right), Union Square (left) and Hotel Continental Saigon standing in front. Vincom Center is standing behind the hotel.)

(Parkson is next to Hotel Continental Saigon (right). Hotel Caravelle (far right) is standing high behind Hotel Continental Saigon.)

(Turn to the left and you will meet a beautiful fountain by Opera House. A Chinese restaurant "泓龍軒 (Dragon Restaurant)" is seen behind the trees on the right.)

(You are looking at Hotel Caravelle Saigon (right) standing on the other side of the road. Pub "Lion" and Korean restaurant "Arirang" are next to the hotel. Chinese restaurant "泓 龍 軒 (Dragon Restaurant)" is standing far left on the photo. A "Highlands Coffee" is sitting on the opposite side of the Chinese restaurant.)

(Hotel Caravelle Saigon)

(Chinese restaurant "泓龍軒 (Dragon Restaurant)" is standing on the left and pub "Lion" is standing on the right. Korean restaurant "Arirang" is next to the pub.)

(Korean restaurant "Arirang" is situated at the same building of pub "Lion".)

(From the Chinese restaurant of "泓 龍 軒 (Dragon Restaurant)", you are looking at "Highlands Coffee". Opera House (far left) is standing by the coffee shop and Park Hyatt Hotel (white) is standing behind the shop.)

(Park Hyatt Hotel. If you follow the road on the photo, you will meet Hotel Continental Saigon next to Park Hyatt.)

(When you pass by the Chinese restaurant towards "Hai Long 5 Hotel" on the street of "Hai Ba Trung", you will meet 3 shops for the replica of sailboat consecutively.)

(They sell various kinds of beautiful sailing boat model.)

(Just before "Highlands Coffee", you are looking back at the fountain by Opera House. Louis Vuitton shop is standing far left on the photo. Rex Hotel (blue) standing at the vast square in front of Ho Chi Minh City Hall, is seen over the fountain.)

(3) Notre Dame Cathedral

If you walk straight from Opera House along "Dong Khoi Road", you will meet Notre Dame Cathedral in around 10 minutes. Notre Dame Cathedral was completed in 1865 as the first cathedral at Ho Chi Minh City. It is considered one of the most beautiful colonial buildings together with City Hall and Central Post Office at the city.

Free entrance and opens to the public twice on weekdays. From 08:00 until 11:00 am and from 3:00 until 4:00 pm. Central Post Office is standing on the left and Diamond Plaza, a shopping mall, is situated behind the cathedral. Reunification Palace, situated to the left, can also be accessed in 10 minutes on foot from Notre Dame Cathedral.

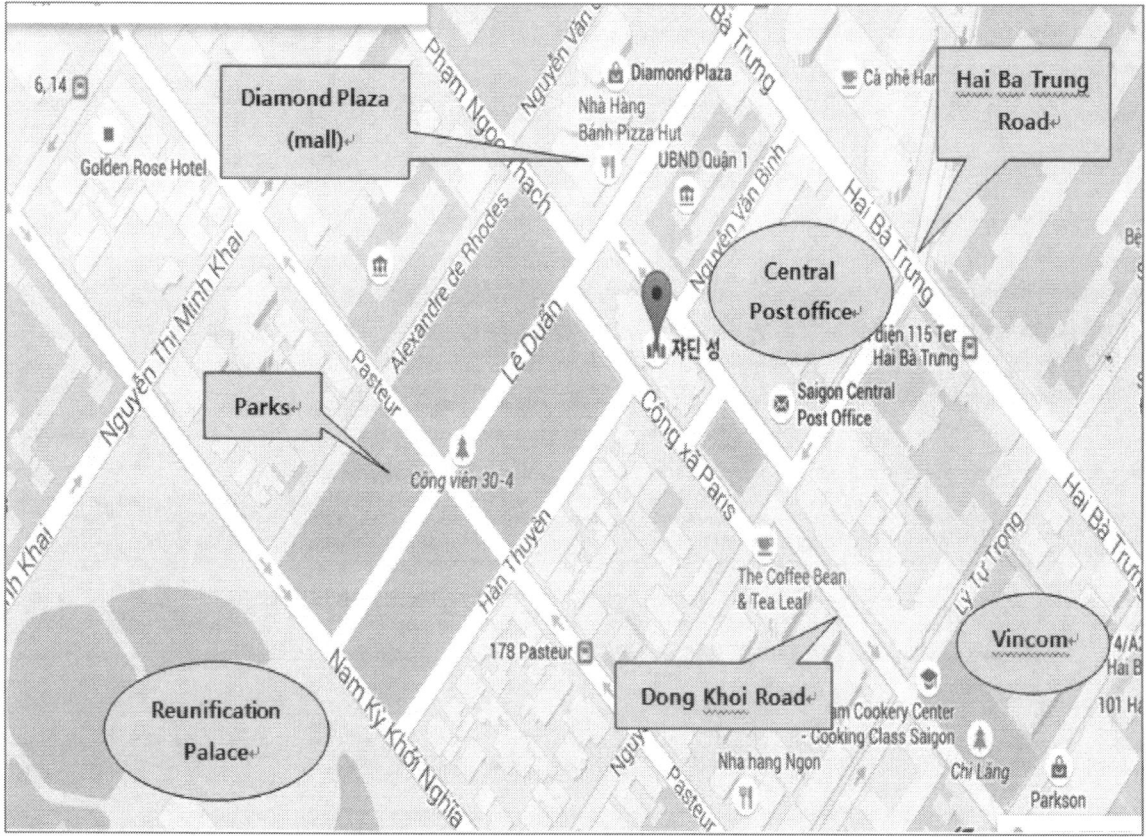

(When you pass by "Vincom Center" along "Dong Khoi Road", you will meet Notre Dame Cathedral shortly. It is standing tall behind a statue of Virgin Mary at the center of a vast rotary. Now, let's go to Notre Dame Cathedral along the road of "Dong Khoi".)

(You are standing in front of Vincom Center. Cross straight like the yellow arrow and you will meet a sign on your left which is standing on the pedestrian way of "Dong Khoi".)

(After Vincom Center (left) standing on the street of "Dong Khoi", you are looking back at the center. Parkson is partly seen behind Vincom Center. Go straight as indicated by the red arrow on the road and you will meet Notre Dam Cathedral in 5 minutes.)

(Just after the crosswalk, you will find this sign on "Dong Khoi Road". Follow the road.)

(Notre Dame Cathedral is partly seen in front.)

(Notre Dame Cathedral. Diamond Plaza (blue) is standing behind the cathedral and Central Post Office is partly seen on the far right on the photo. For Reunification Palace, you have to cross the road to the left.)

(Another gorgeous colonial structure, "Central Post Office", is situated on the other side of the road.)

(Inside cathedral. Open to the public twice on weekdays. From 08:00 until 11:00 am and from 3:00 until 4:00 pm.)

(A statue of Virgin Mary is standing in front of Notre Dame Cathedral.)

(From cathedral, you are looking back at the road of "Dong Khoi". Vincom Center is standing tall left and HSBC (dome) is on the right.)

(Inside cathedral)

(4) Central Post Office

Central Post Office, one of the most beautiful colonial buildings at Ho Chi Minh City, was designed by Gustav Eiffel who also drew the blueprint of Eiffel Tower in Paris. When you enter the office, you will meet a huge portrait of Ho Chi Minh hung high on the opposite wall. Except postcards and a souvenir shop, antique old telephone booths are also preserved well in the office. Travelers and people who send letters and parcels are crowded all day long.

(Central Post Office)

(Inside Central Post Office. A big portrait of Ho Chi Minh is hung on the wall.)

(A souvenir shop surrounded by counters is located at the center of the hall.)

(Antique telephone booths are on both sides of inside Central Post Office.)

(You are looking back at the entrance. Why don't you take a break at this wide and cool office? Here take a brief look at "Diamond Plaza", a shopping mall with a food court, next.)

(Diamond Plaza)

A giant shopping mall, "Diamond Plaza", is situated behind Notre Dame Cathedral. Except malls, it has a food court and a mart at the 4th floor. It's one of places for taking a rest after Notre Dame Cathedral, Central Post Office or Reunification Palace.

("Diamond Plaza" behind the cathedral.)

(A food court at the 4th level of the mall.)

(5) Reunification Palace

Reunification Palace is located around 10-minute-walk away from Notre Dame Cathedral. It was used as Presidential Palace before reunification of Vietnam. It opens twice a day. From 07:30 am until 12:00 pm and from 13:00 until 17:00 pm. No admission after 11:00 am and after 16:00 pm. Admission fee is VND30,000.

When you enter the gate, you will find 2 tanks displayed on the right side of the vast park prepared in front of the palace. They are the tanks which forced into the former Presidential Palace on 30 April 1975. They were considered as the vanguard for Reunification of Vietnam. You will also take a look at the heliport where the last U.S. helicopter escaped Ho Chi Minh City, formerly known as "Saigon". After the exhibition halls, do not pass by the bunker preserved at the basement.

(Reunification Palace. 2 tanks are displayed on the right. Now, let's go from Notre Dame Cathedral to Reunification Palace.)

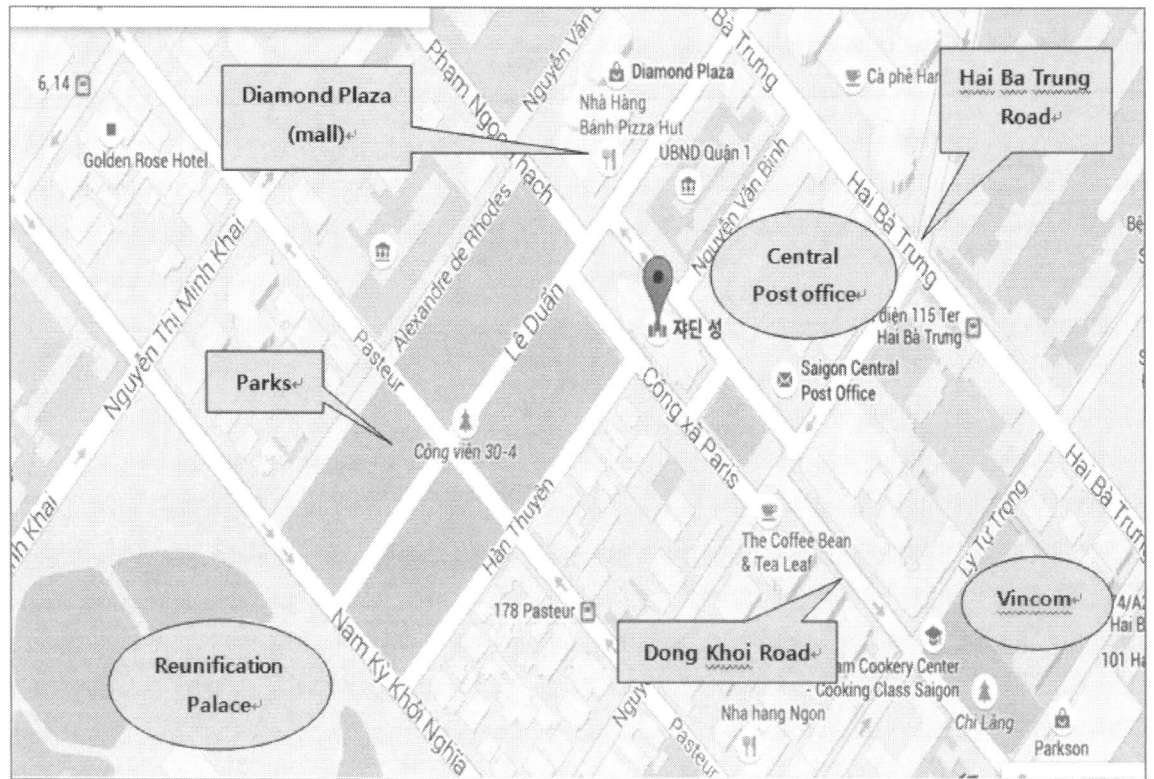

(Notre Dame Cathedral is indicated by a red mark on the map. When you stand in front of the cathedral, cross the road to the left. Then, you will meet a wide park. Reunification Palace is situated at the end of the park.)

(At Notre Dame Cathedral partly seen on the far right, cross the road to the left as indicated by the yellow arrow on the photo.)

(After crossing the road, you are looking back at Notre Dame Cathedral from the park.)

(Reunification Palace is standing at the end of the park. If you come from Notre Dame Cathedral, you may walk the park seen on the left.)

(Near Reunification Palace.)

(Ticket office is on the left. VND30,000.)

(You are looking back at the road you've just passed through.)

(Reunification Palace)

(There is a vast park in front of Reunification Palace.)

(The tanks are displayed on a side of the park.)

(Inside Reunification Palace.)

(A reception hall.)

394

(Another one.)

(Information boards)

(Another reception hall.)

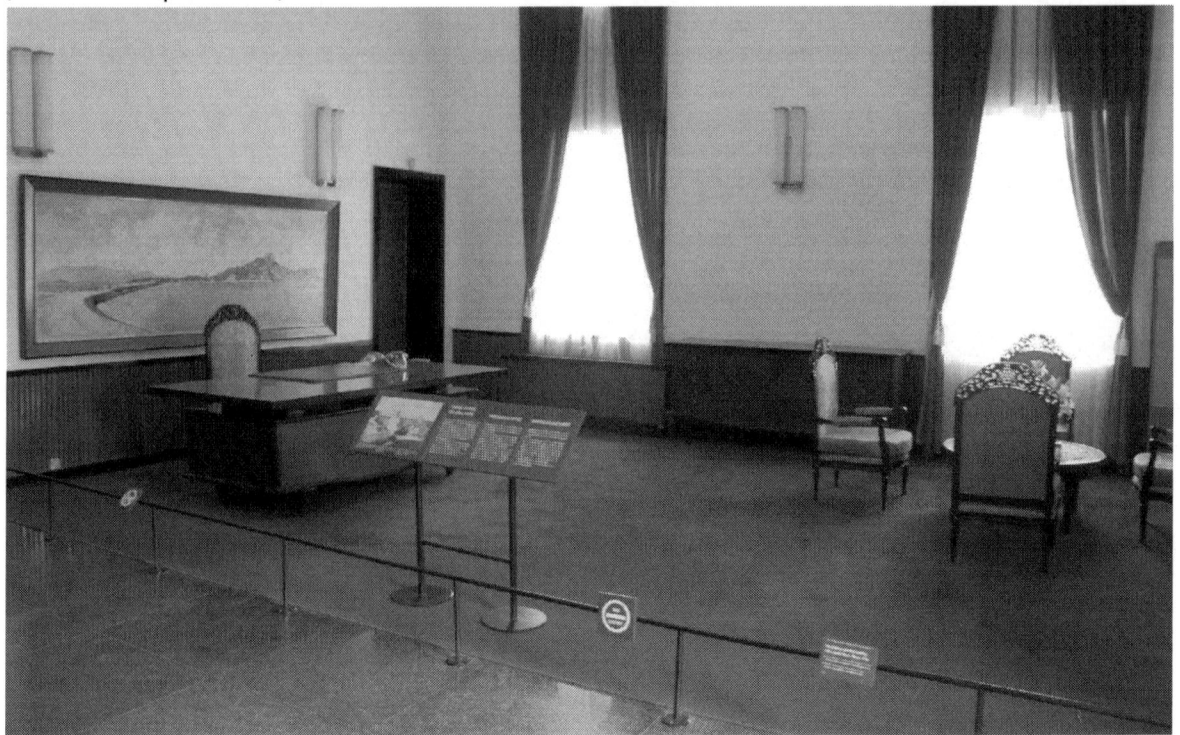

(Presidential Office. The information board standing at the office says "Nguyen Van Thieu", former president of Southern Vietnam, was born in 1923 and died in Boston, USA, in 2001.")

(Command Center in the bunker of Reunification Palace.)

(Visitors are taking photos at a communication center of the bunker.)

(6) Ben Thanh Market

Ben Thanh Market is a big traditional market located near city center of Ho Chi Minh City. It opened since 1920 and takes around 15 minutes from Opera House along the road of "Le Loi". It has a big clock on its head.

Ben Thanh Bus Station is also situated on the opposite side of the road, where you can take buses for airport and China Town. If you walk around 10 minutes from the market, you can also get "De Tham Road" known as a travelers' street in 10 minutes.

(At the end of the road of "Le Loi", you will meet Ben Thanh Market on the right. Ben Thanh Bus Station is located on the other side of the road.)

(Way from Opera House to Bin Thanh Market.)

When you stand at Opera House, you will see Union Square on your right and a Louis Vuitton shop on your left. It is "Le Loi Road" lying between the 2 luxurious shopping malls. However, the wide road towards Ben Thanh Market, is temporarily blocked by fence due to the construction of subway. Therefore, you have to use a narrow path prepared by Union Square. Let's take a look at the map in advance.

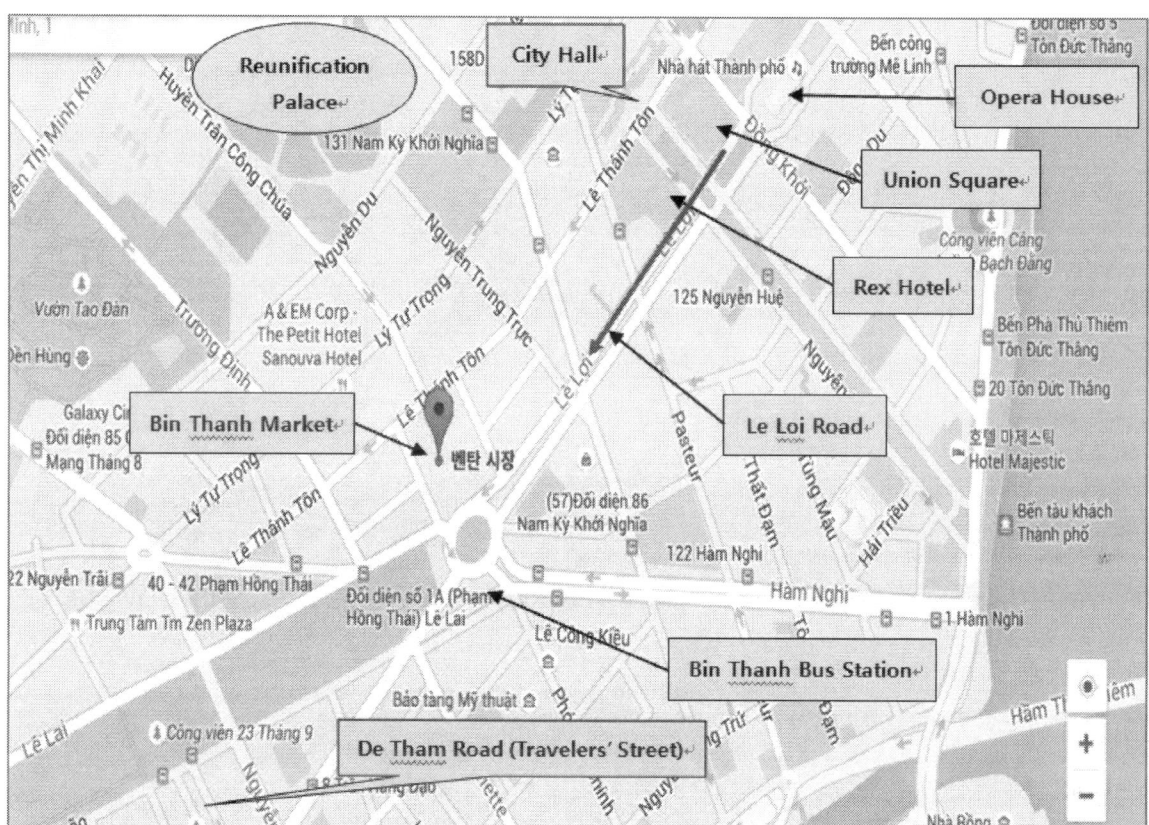

(Go through the narrow path by Union Square and you will meet Rex Hotel at the vast square where Ho Chi Minh Statue is standing. Then, you will find another narrow path in front of the hotel. "Le Loi Road" at the hotel is also temporarily blocked due to the metro construction.

Pass by Rex Hotel through the narrow path and the road gets wide. Go straight along the road of "Le Loi" for 5 minutes and you will meet "Ben Thanh Market" standing on the right. You will also easily find "Ben Thanh Bus Station" on the opposite side of a vast rotary.

Now, let's take a look at another 2 maps one by one which are enlarged for the road of "Le Loi" from Opera House to Ben Thanh Market.)

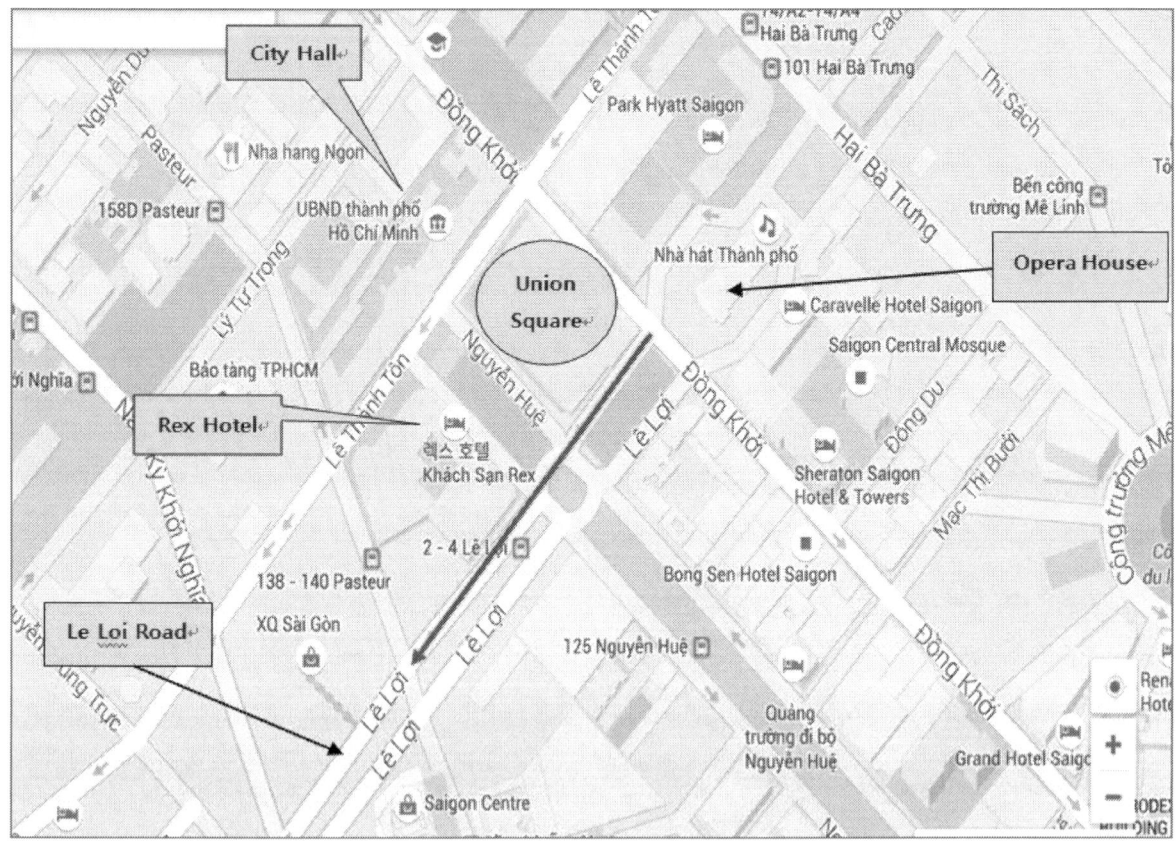

(This is a map enlarged for "Le Loi Road" from Opera House. Follow straight as indicated by the red arrow on the map. As explained earlier, the road of "Le Loi" between Union Square and Rex Hotel is under construction for the first metro at Ho Chi Minh City. Therefore, you have to use the narrow paths temporarily prepared by the mall and the hotel. Here shows you another enlarged map for the road of "Le Loi" from Rex Hotel to Ben Thanh Market next.)

(From Ben Thanh Bus Station, you are looking at Ben Thanh Market with a clock on its head.)

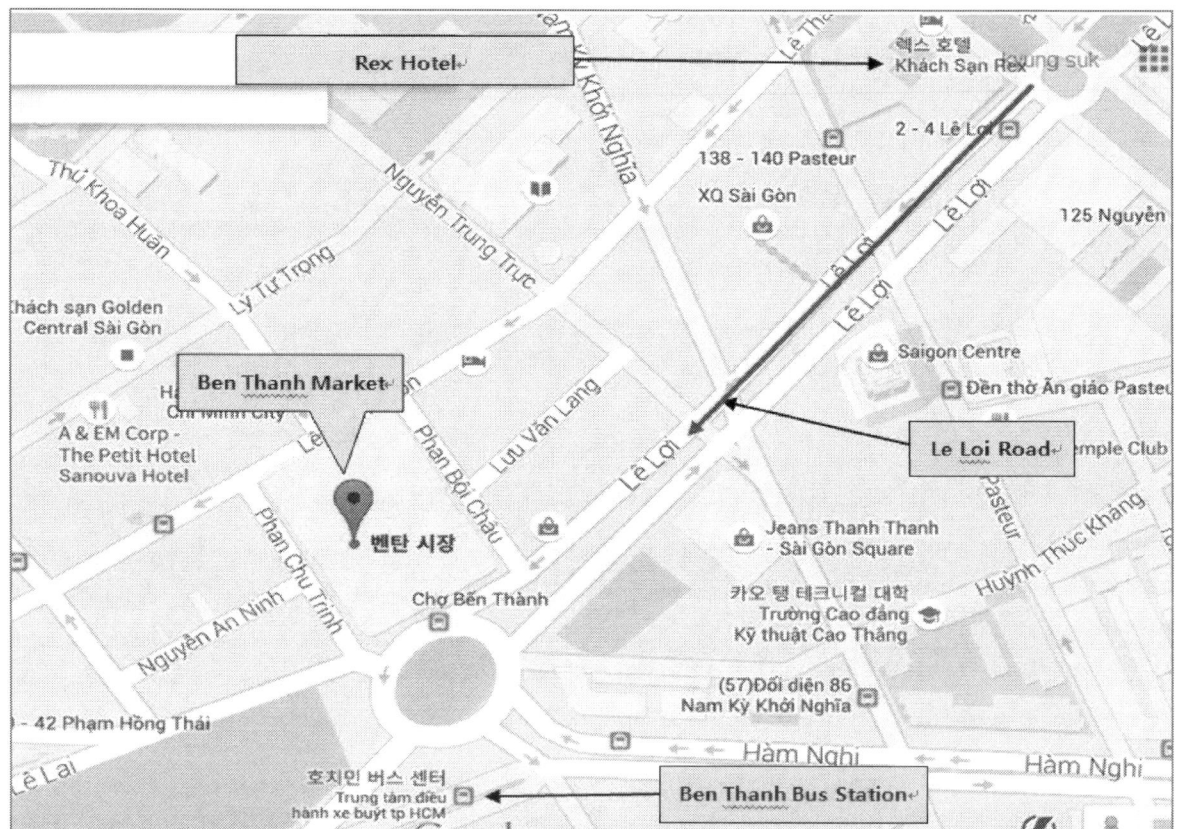

(Pass by Rex Hotel through a narrow path and the road will get wide. Keep going straight along "Le Loi Road" and you will shortly meet the market on your right. Over the wide rotary, you will find Ben Thanh Bus Station. Then, let's start from Opera House at city center to Ben Thanh Market.)

(Opera House. Stand in front of the entrance with your back to the house and you will find Union Square on the right and Louis Vuitton shop on the left.)

(From Opera House, you are looking at Union Square. A wide road of "Le Loi" between Union Square and Louis Vuitton shop is temporarily closed except a narrow path prepared by Union Square. Follow the yellow arrow on the photo and you will meet the narrow path for pedestrians.)

(From Union Square, you are looking back at Opera House.)

(After the narrow path by Union Square (right), you are looking at Ho Chi Minh City Hall standing on the right. You will go to another narrow path at Rex Hotel (left).)

(The wide road of "Le Loi" is temporarily closed by a fence due to subway construction. Follow the yellow arrow on the photo and you will meet another narrow path prepared just in front of "Chanel" shop on the ground floor of Rex Hotel.)

(You are going to the narrow path prepared in front of "Chanel" shop at Rex Hotel.)

(Pass through the narrow path and the road of "Le Loi" becomes wide.)

(After the narrow path at Rex Hotel, you are looking at "Saigon Square" on the other side of the road of "Le Loi". Cars are running by "Saigon Square", a shopping mall. Go straight as indicated by a yellow arrow on the photo. Then, you will meet Ben Thanh Market in 3 minutes.)

(At the end of the road of "Le Loi", you will meet Ben Thanh Market on the right. Ben Thanh Bus Station is located on the other side of the road.)

(The other side of Ben Thanh Market.)

(Shoes, bags, accessories, foods. Nearly nothing not found.)

(Every alley is filled with stacks of goods.)

(Clothes)

(You are looking back at one of exits of Bin Thanh Market.)

(7) Fine Arts Museum

This museum consists of 2 galleries. One has drawings some related with socialist and war, the other hall exhibits special paintings by contemporary artists. It is located around 5-minute-walk from Ben Thanh Bus Station. VND10,000.

(Fine Art Museum)

(Way from Ben Thanh Bus Station to "Fine Arts Museum".)

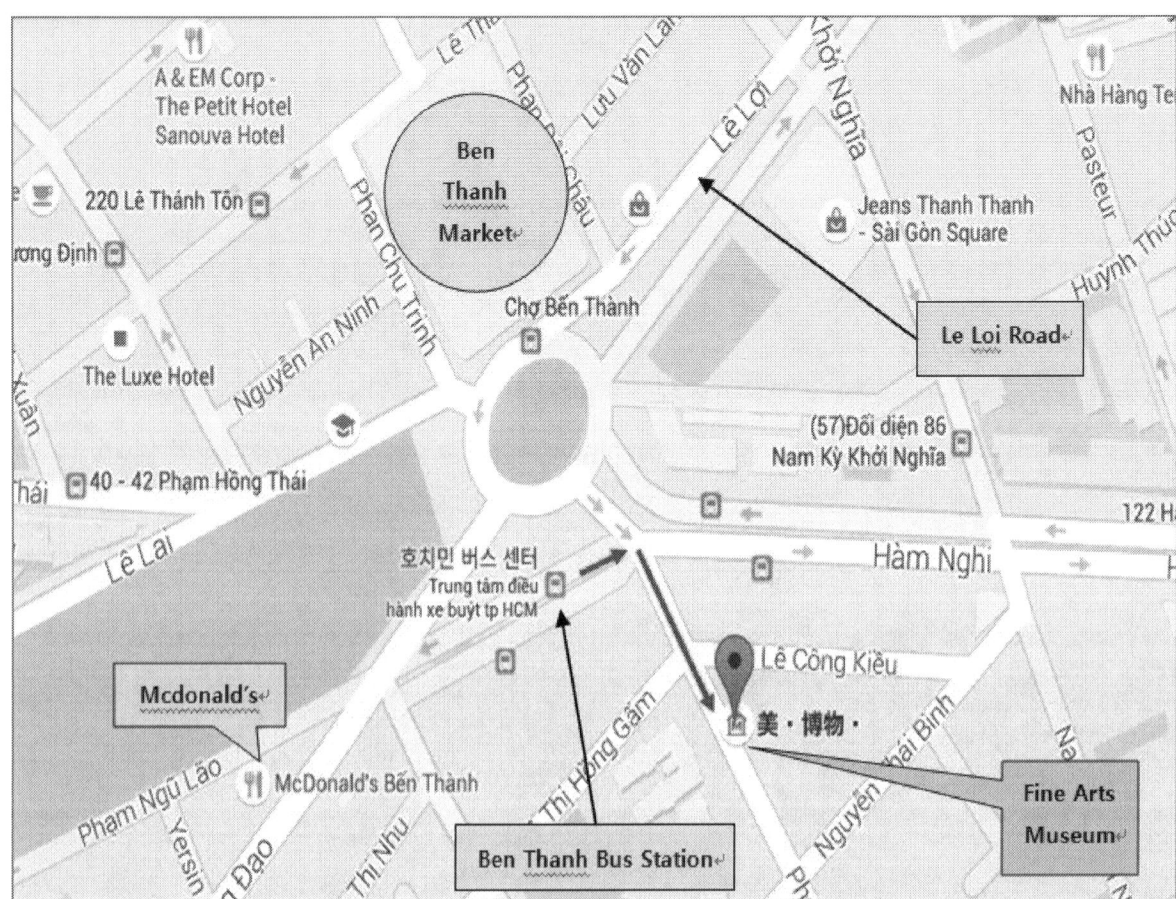

(If you arrive at Ben Thanh Bus Station by bus, you will find a Mcdonald's standing by a park. Then, come out of the terminal to the opposite direction of the fast food store. And, turn to the right along the road of "Puo Duc Chinh". Then, you will meet "Fine Arts Museum in 3 minutes. The red arrows on the map are shown your way from Ben Thanh Bus Station to the museum.)

(Ben Thanh Bus Station. A bus seen on the left has just arrived at the terminal. Follow the yellow arrow on the photo.)

(When you arrive at Ben Thanh Bus Station by bus, follow the arrow.)

(When you come out of Ben Thanh Bus Station, you will meet the 3-story-building of "Saigon Railway Passenger Transport Co." standing on the left. "Rolex" (white) is standing on the right.)

(Turn to the right as indicated by a yellow arrow on the photo. It's "Pho Duc Chinh Road".)

("Highlands Coffee" is situated at the beginning of "Pho Duc Chinh Road". Fine Arts Museum is located around 100 meters away from here.)

(Fine Arts Museum.)

(They have 2 kinds of gallery. Admission fee is VND10,000.)

(Main exhibition hall. Deposit your luggage in the cabinet. Taking photos available.)

(Exhibition hall)

(Paintings and sculpture)

415

(Oil painting)

(A soldier is showing the portrait of Ho Chi Minh.)

416

(Warriors are sailing on the river.)

(Drawings displayed in the special exhibition hall which is prepared at the other house.)

(A place to take a rest is prepared between exhibition halls on the 2nd floor.)

(8) De Tham Road (Travelers' Street)

De Tam Road has many cheap hotels, pubs, restaurants and travel agencies. It is worth to be called as a travelers' street. It takes around 20 minutes on foot from city center where many attractions are concentrated such as City Hall and Opera House. If you walk from Ben Thanh Bus Station, it would take around 15 minutes. Considering that there also are many cheap and clean hotels at city center, you'd better book a hotel near Opera House and take a look at De Tam Road as an attraction of Ho Chi Minh City.

Here introduce the way from Ben Thanh Bus Station to De Tam Road via a Mcdonald's, which is standing between Ben Thanh Market and the travelers' street.

(De Tham Road. A tour bus run by "the Sinh Tourist", a famous travel agency in Vietnam, is waiting for travelers for outskirts of Ho Chi Minh City.)

(Way from Ben Thanh Bus Station to De Tam Road.)

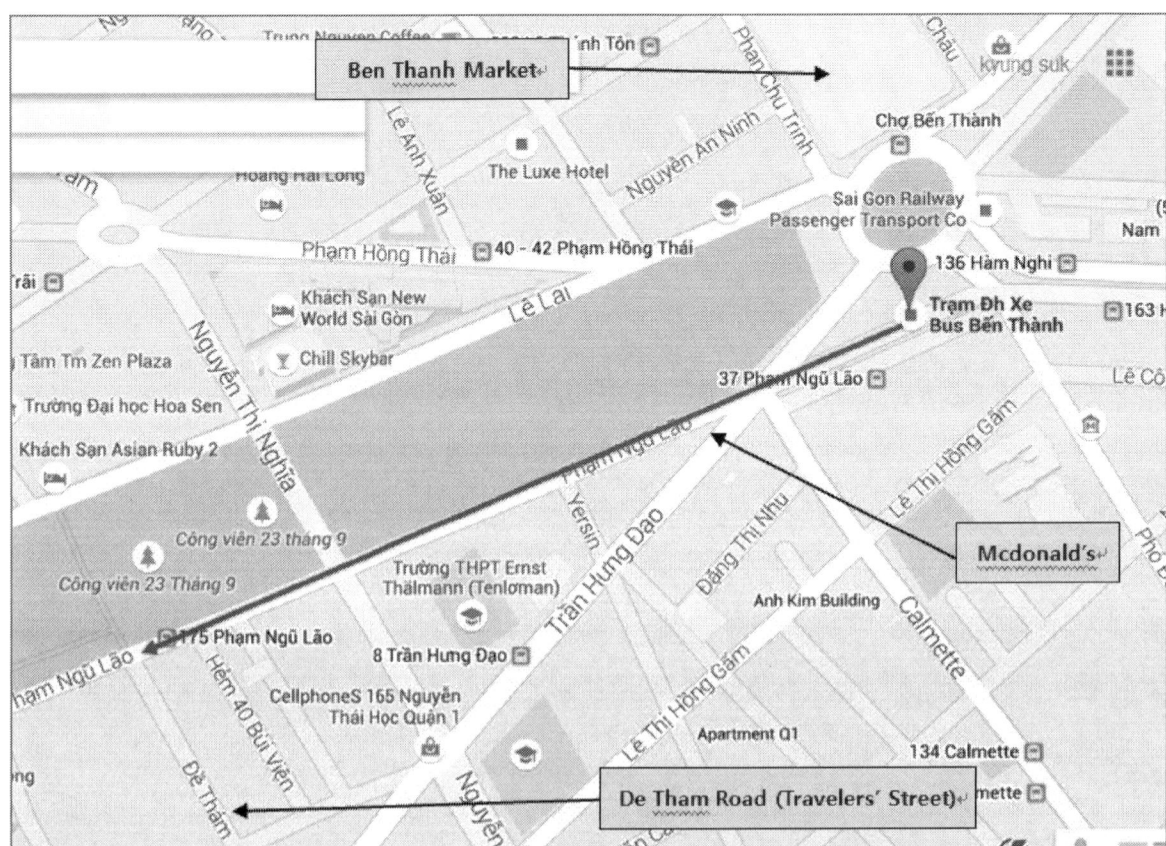

(When you arrive at Ben Thanh Bus Station by bus, you will easily find a long park, where a Mcdonald's is standing near the park. Go straight along the parks as indicated by the red arrow from Ben Thanh Bus Station. Then, you will find the gate to De Tam Road in 15 minutes. You can also take a rest at the cool fast food store on the way to the travelers' street.)

(Ben Thanh Bus Station. In case of bus, you will arrive at here. Follow the yellow arrow on the photo. It's the opposite direction of Fine Arts Museum.)

(From Ben Thanh Bus Station, you are looking at a Mcdonald's near the park on the right. Take the pedestrian way by the park seen on the right.)

(Take the road on the right. Follow the yellow arrow on the photo and you will meet a crossroads in 5 minutes. Cross the junction straight and keep walking along the park. Then, you will find an arch prepared on the left side of the road. It's the entrance to "De Tam Road".)

(A pup "Seventeen Saloon (Heineken)" is standing on the other side of the road on the way to De Tam Road.)

(You are looking back at Mcdonald's before crossroads.)

(Cross this junction straight and go straight around 100 meters. Then, you will find an arch standing on the left side of the road. "De Tam Road" is situated in the area seen on the left.)

(Can you see the gate on the other side the road? It's the beginning of the travelers' street.)

(De Tam Road, a travelers' street.)

(A tour bus on De Tam Road.)

(Pubs are lined up by the street.)

(Hotels and restaurants in the alley.)

(Shops, pubs, restaurants and travel agencies.)

(9) Mariamman Hindu Temple

It's a traditional Hindu temple built in the 19th century. Goddess Mariamman gives abundance and fertilization, they believe. Free entrance and off between 12:00 pm and 13:30 pm.

(Mariamman Hindu Temple. It's near from Ben Thanh Market.)

(Way from city center to Mariamman Hindu Temple)

When you come to the temple from city center, go straight along the road of "Ly Tu Trong", which is lying in front of Vincom Center at city center. Mariamman Hindu Temple is located around 500 meters away from Vincom Center. Let's take a look at the map below.

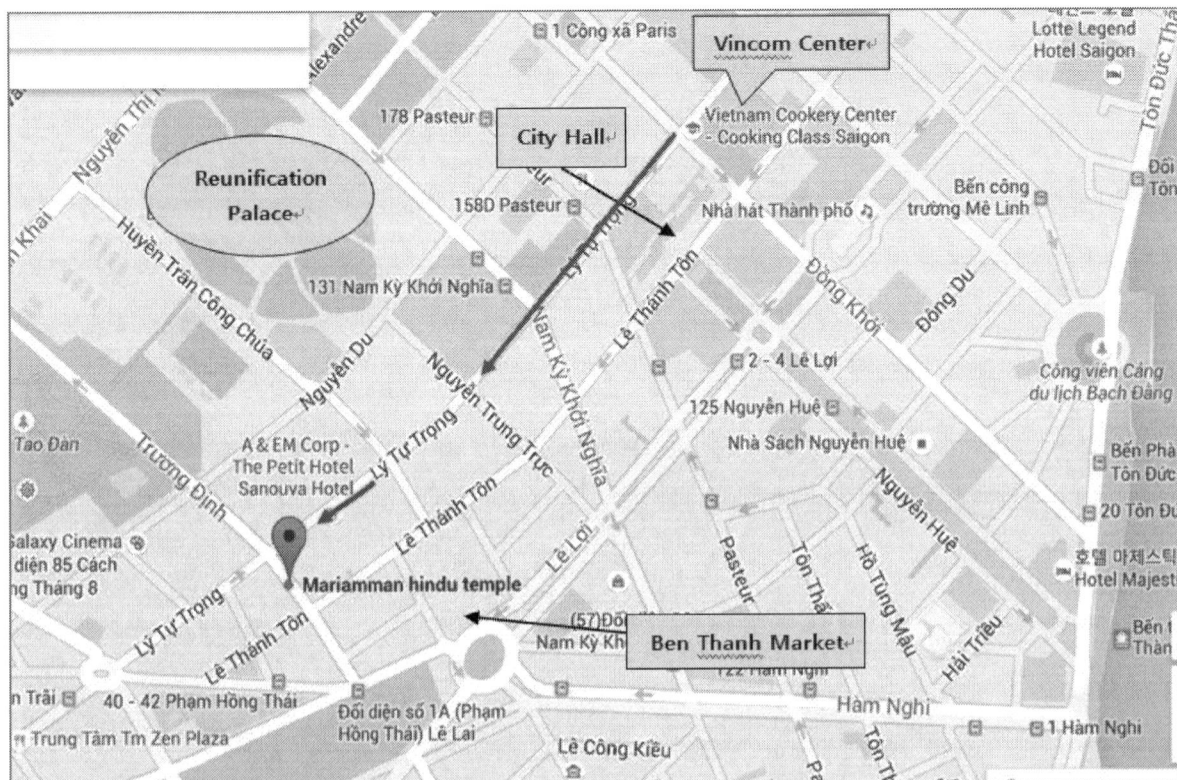

(Take the way of "Ly Tu Trong" as indicated by the red arrows on the map. Then, you will find Ben Thanh Market first which is standing at the end of an alley to the left. It's around 400 meters from Vincom Center. Mariamman Hindu Temple is situated in the other alley next to the market. Now, let's go from Vincom Center to the temple along "Ly Tu Trong Road".)

(You are looking at the main entrance to Vincom Center (blue) which is standing on the left. Follow the yellow arrow on the photo. It's "Ly Tu Trong Road".)

("Ly Tu Trong Road". Go straight around 500 meters.)

(When you pass by this park, you will find Ho Chi Minh City Museum on the other side of the road.)

(Ho Chi Minh City Museum)

(On the way to Mariamman Hindu Temple along the road of "Ly Tu Trong", you will find Ben Thanh Market first, which is standing at the end of an alley on the left. It's around 400 meters away from Vincom Center. Mariamman Hindu Temple is located next alley.)

(Mariamman Hindu Temple is partly seen at the alley where motorbikes are running out.)

(Mariamman Hindu Temple)

(Prayers are preparing incense to burn.)

(Take off your shoes inside.)

(10) Saigon Riverside

There is a long promenade by the Saigon River which is located around 10-minute-walk away from Opera House at city center. You will meet people playing badminton or exercising at the promenade early in the morning. There you can also meet a pier for boat tour.

When you come to the river along the road of "Hai Ba Trung" from city center, you will meet a statue of General Tran Hung Dao standing close to the river. He is a hero who defeated Mongolian invasion in the 13th century. A shrine dedicated to him will be introduced in detail later.

A luxurious hotel of "Majestic" and a tasty Korean BBQ restaurant of "Choi Go Jip" are situated near the river. Here introduces the way to Saigon Riverside from "Hai Long 5 Hotel" on "Hai Ba Trung Road". It takes only 5 minutes on foot.

(Saigon Riverside Promenade)

434

(Way to Saigon Riverside through "Hai Ba Trung Road")

It's very easy to get the Saigon Riverside from city center. If you follow "Hai Ba Trung Road" as indicated by the red arrow on the map below, you will meet the statue of General Tran Hung Dao shortly, which is standing at a rotary by the riverside.

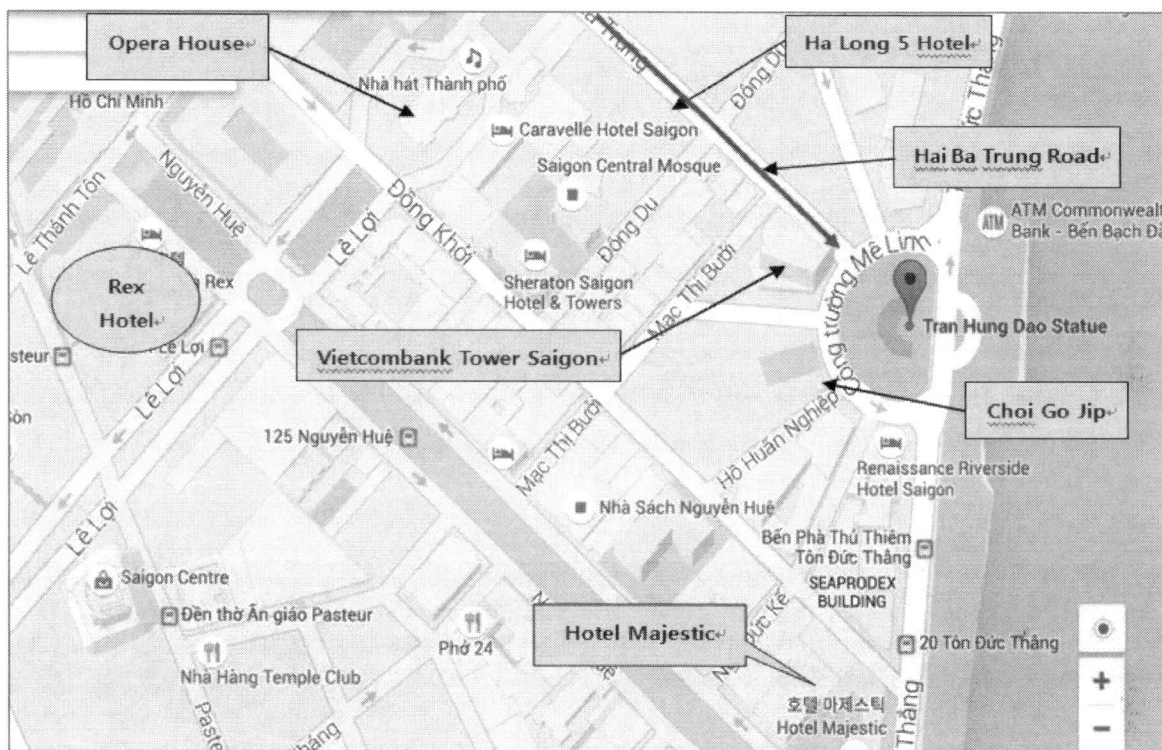

(You will meet "Vietcombank Tower Saigon" on your right when you stand at the end of the road of "Hai Ba Trung", which is indicated by the red arrow on the map. Korean BBQ restaurant "Choi Go Jip" is located near the tower. When you take a stroll on the riverside promenade, you will meet "Hotel Majestic" on the other side of the road.)

(From Vietcombank Tower at the end of "Hai Ba Trung Road", you are looking at the statue of General Tran Hung Dao. The statue is looking down on the Saigon River.)

Restaurant "Choi Go Jip

(You are looking back at Korean restaurant "Choi Go Jip" on the way to the Saigon River.)

(From Saigon Riverside Promenade, you are looking at the statue of General Tran Jung Dao. "Vietcombank Tower Saigon" is standing behind the statue.)

(They are playing badminton at Saigon Riverside Promenade early in the morning.)

(Saigon Riverside Promenade)

(Saigon River. A ticket box for boat tour is located on the left.)

(Ticket box for boat tour.)

(An office for Saigon Restaurant ship is situated at the promenade, too.)

(From Saigon Riverside Promenade, you are looking at Hotel Majestic on the other side of the road.)

(Hotel Majestic. It lights its body with beautiful colors at night.)

(11) China Town (Binh Tay Market, Cha Tam Church, Ong Bon Pagoda (二府廟))

China Town is located around 30 minutes away from city center by bus. Binh Tay Market, the biggest market in Ho Chi Minh City, Cha Tam Church and Ong Bon Pagoda are the attractions at the town. They are situated near "Cho Lon Bus Station" which is the final destination of bus No. 1 departing from Ben Thanh Bus Station.

("Cha Tam Church". 5 minutes of foot from "Cho Lon Bus Station".)

(A Chinese assembly hall and a shrine, "Ong Bon Pagoda". 10 minutes from the bus terminal.)

(Way from Ben Thanh Bus Station to China Town.)

It takes around 30 minutes by bus from Ben Thanh Bus Station to Cho Lon Bus Station. Take a bus No. 1 from Ben Thanh Bus Station and get off the bus at its final destination. It's Cho Lon Bus Station.

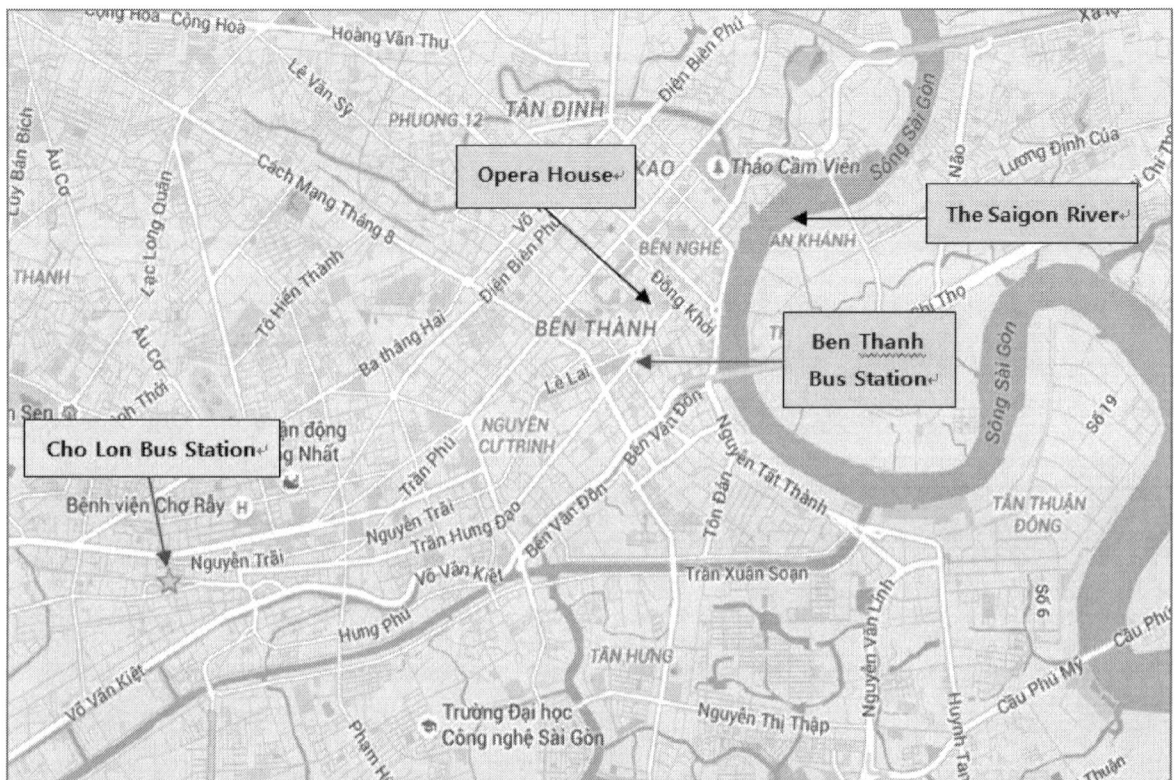

(Binh Tay Market, Cha Tam Church and Ong Bon Pagoda are all situated near Cho Lon Bus Station. Let's take a look at the other map enlarged for the bus station at China Town.)

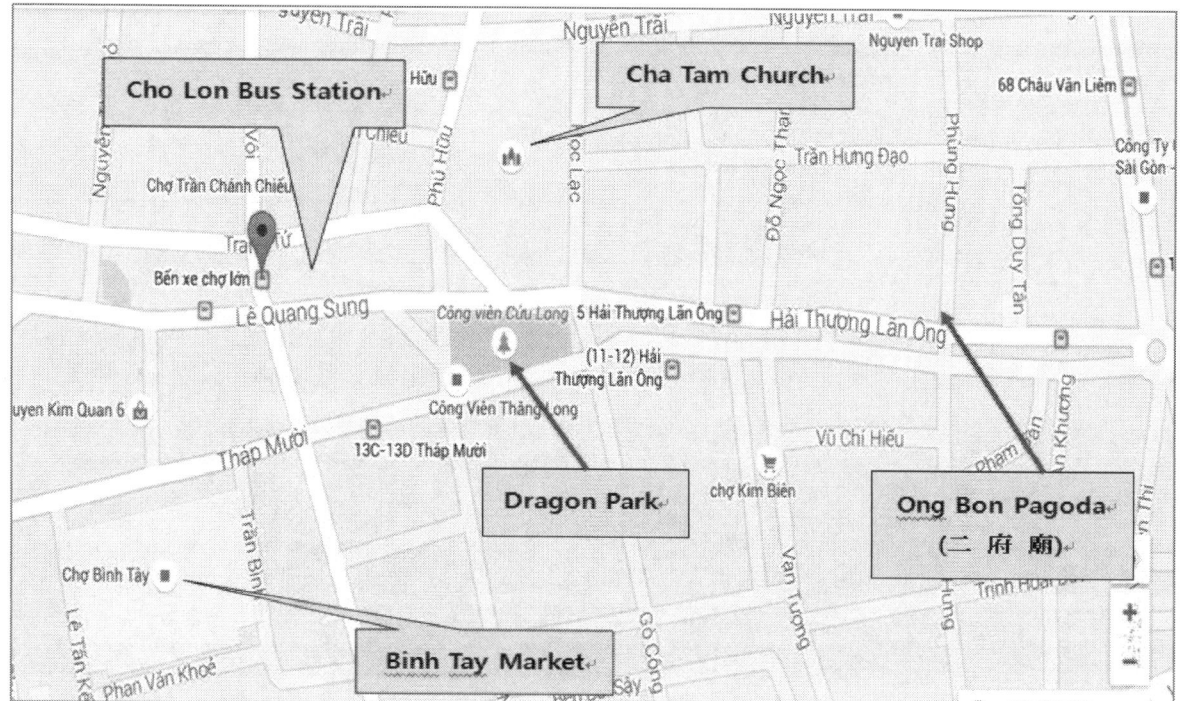

(When you arrive at Cho Lon Bus Station, look back and you will find a church spire. It's "Cha Tam Church. It takes not more than 10 minutes on foot from Cho Lon Bus Station to the church.

After Cha Tam Church, take the road of "Hai Thuong Lan Ong" and you will meet "Ong Bon Pagoda (二 府 廟) in 10 minutes.

For Binh Tay Market, come out of Cho Lon Bus Station through the gate where buses are coming out. And go down 1 block and you will find the big market on the left.)

(Bus No. 1 bound for "Cho Lon Bus Station". It costs VND5,000 and cool.)

(Cho Lon Bus Station. Buses are arriving through this gate. The departure gate is located on the other side of the bus terminal.)

(Cho Lon Bus Station. You've just got off the bus No. 1 seen left. When you are going to Binh Tay Market, go straight this way and you will meet the departure gate for buses. At the departure gate, take the way to the left.)

Cha Tam Church

(Look back and you will find a church spire standing far away. It's Cha Tam Church. For this church, go this way straight and you will find a small gate on your right. You will also find the arrival gate on the left. Now, let's take a look at the attractions at China Town one by one.)

(Binh Tay Market)

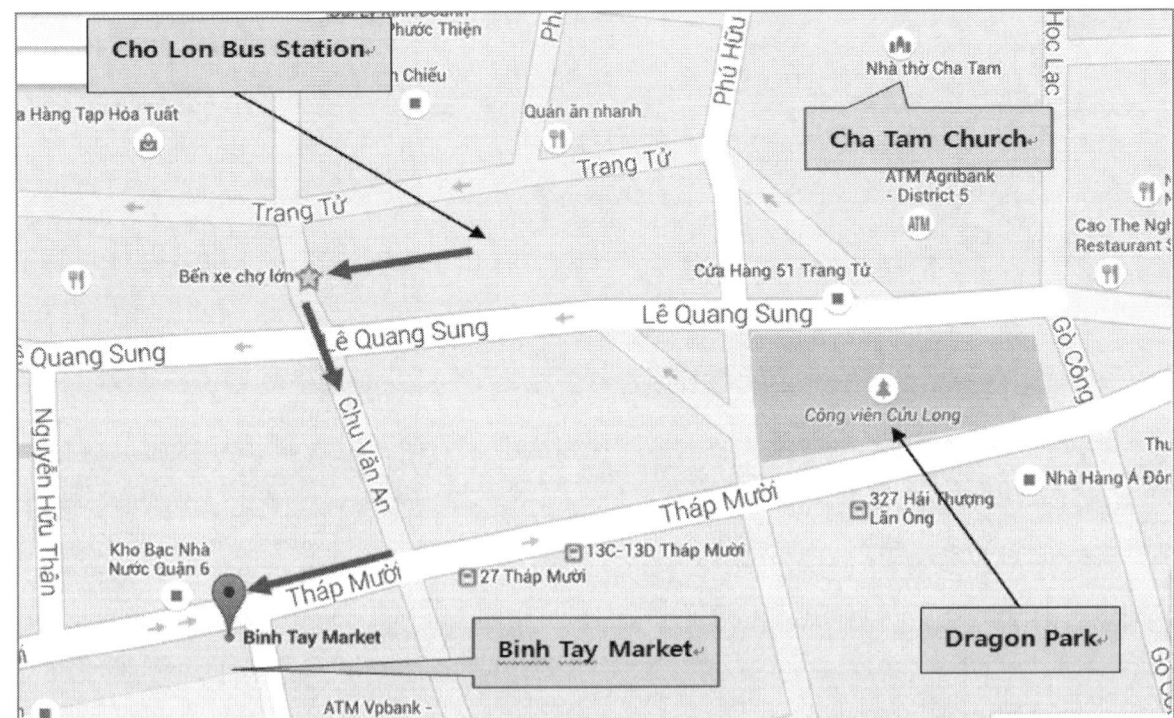

(At the vast bus terminal of "Cho Lon", come out of the departure gate and turn to the left as indicated by the 2nd red arrow on the map. Turn to the right like the 3rd arrow and you will meet Binh Tay Market shortly.)

(Binh Tay Market. It takes around 15 minutes on foot from Cho Lon Bus Station.)

(Cha Tam Church)

(Cha Tam Church (方濟各天主堂))

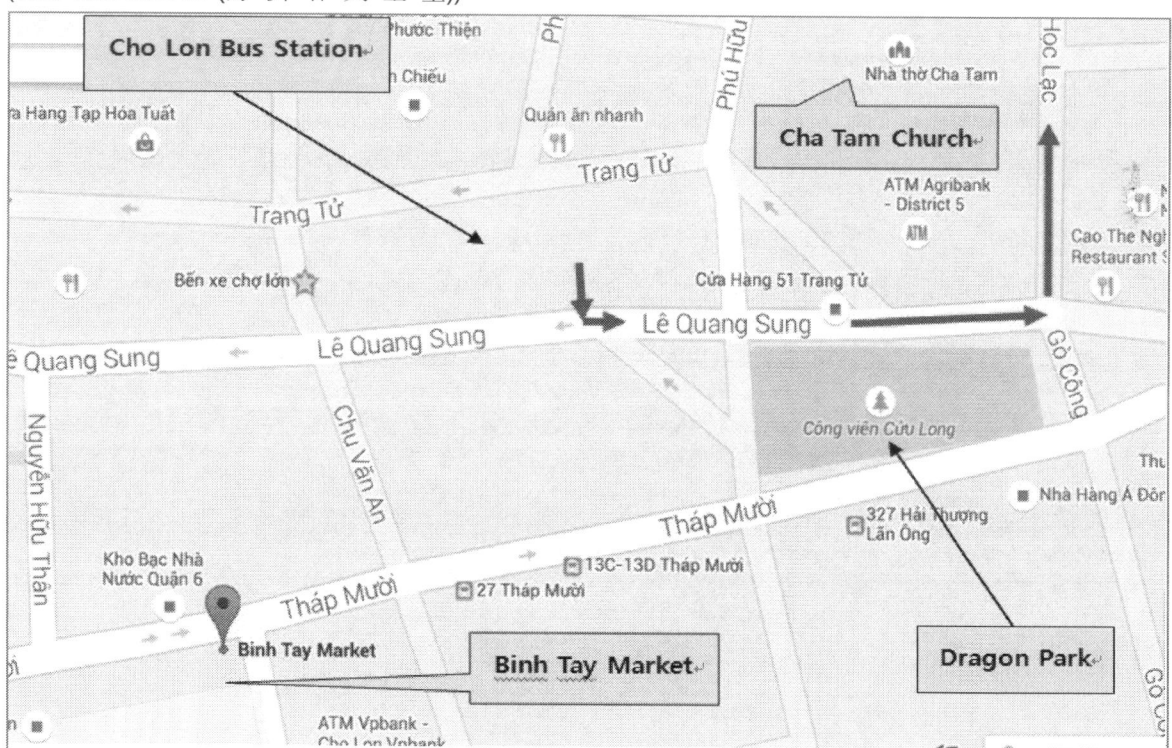

(After alighting from the bus, find a small gate located on the opposite side of the arrival gate and come out of the gate as indicated by the 1st and 2nd red arrows on the map. It's the street of "Le Quang Sung". Go straight the road with "Dragon Park" on your right. Just at the end of the park, you will find an alley to the left. Cha Tam Church is situated 100 meters away on the left.)

(This is the arrival gate to Cho Lon Bus Station. The small gate towards "Le Quang Sung Road" is prepared on the opposite side of the arrival gate. A red arrow indicates the small gate for the road. Come out of the small gate and turn to the left.)

(As indicated by the yellow arrow on the photo, go straight along the street of "Le Quang Sung Road", where motorbikes are running. A dragon park is seen on the opposite side of the road.)

(At the end of the dragon park, you will shortly meet an alley to the left, which is seen in front. Cha Tam Church is standing around 100 meters away in the alley.)

(Cha Tam Church 方濟各天主堂)

(Cha Tam Church)

(Inside church)

(You are looking back at the entrance to the church.)

(Ong Bon Pagoda (二 府 廟. Mieu Nhi Phu.))

("Ong Bon Pagoda (二 府 廟. Mieu Nhi Phu)" is a Chinese assembly hall and a shrine.)

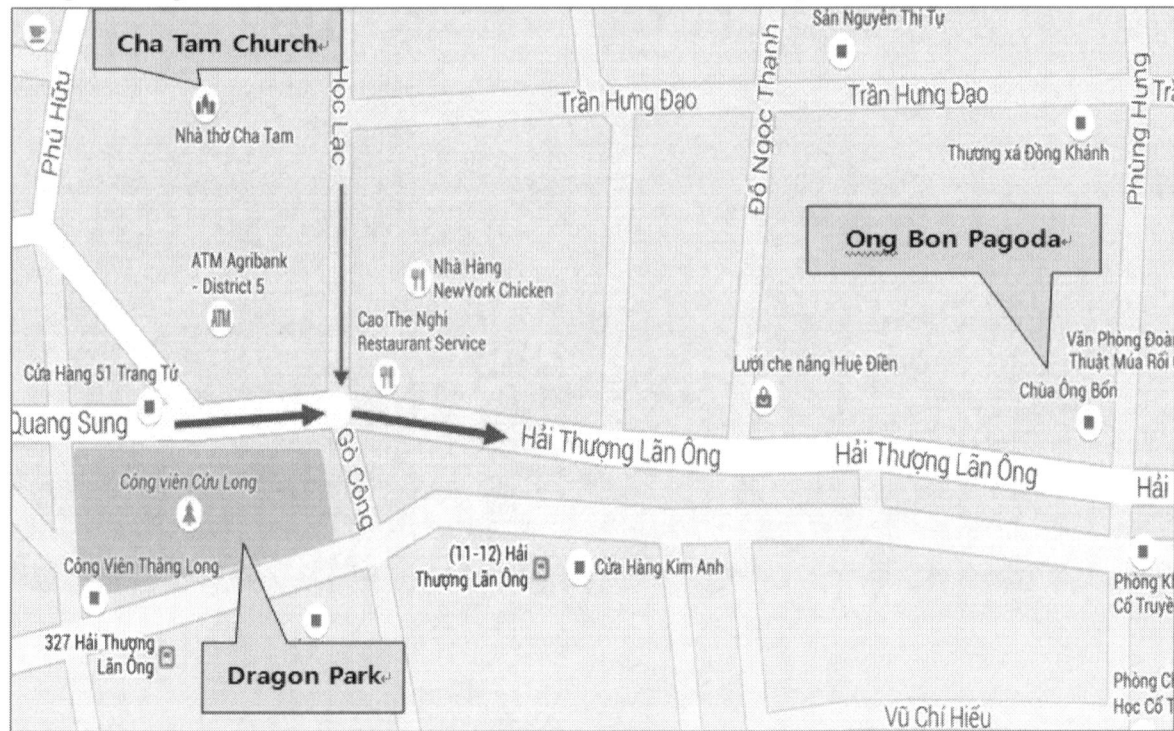

(After Cha Tam Church, follow the street of "Le Quang Sung" as indicated by the red arrows on map. And you will meet "Ong Bon Pagoda" in 5 minutes.)

(After coming out of the alley to "Cha Tam Church" and go to the left along "Le Quang Sung Road" as indicated by the yellow arrow on the photo. Ong Bon Pagoda is standing left 200 meters away.)

(Ong Bon Pagoda (二 府 廟. Mieu Nhi Phu))

(Ong Bon Pagoda)

("二府會館" is a Chinese assembly hall.)

(Burning incense.)

("福 佑 興 隆" means "Fortune and Prosperity".)

(12) Le Van Tam Park & Tran Hung Dao Temple

"Le Van Tam Park" is located near "Tran Hung Dao Temple". When you come to this temple along the street of "Hai Ba Trung" from city center, you will have to pass by or through the park. The temple is dedicated to the legendary general of "Tran Hung Dao" who defeated Mongolian invasion in 1287. You can also remember his statue standing by the Saigon River. Free admission to the temple. You will also meet many people exercising at the park early in the morning.

(Tran Hung Dao Temple)

(Way from City Center to Tran Hung Dao Temple via Le Van Tam Park.)

It's easy to get Le Van Tam Park. Only follow the street of "Hai Ba Trung" around 500 meters from "Hai Long 5 Hotel" as shown on the map below. Then, you will meet the park on the right. If you follow the second red arrow, you will meet the temple shortly.

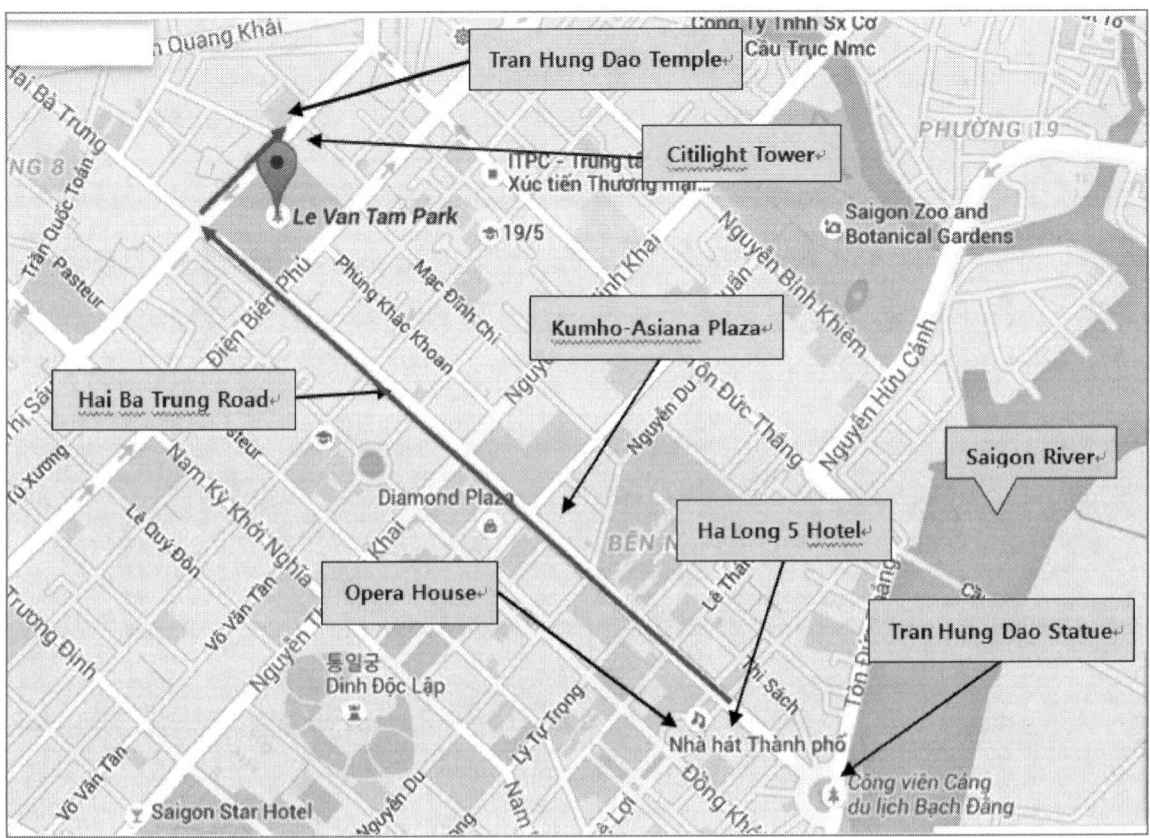

(After Le Van Tam Park, when you go to Tran Hung Dao Temple, you will meet Citilight Tower on your right. From the tall building, Tran Hung Dao Temple is standing on the other side of the road. Let's see an enlarged map around Le Van Tam Park.)

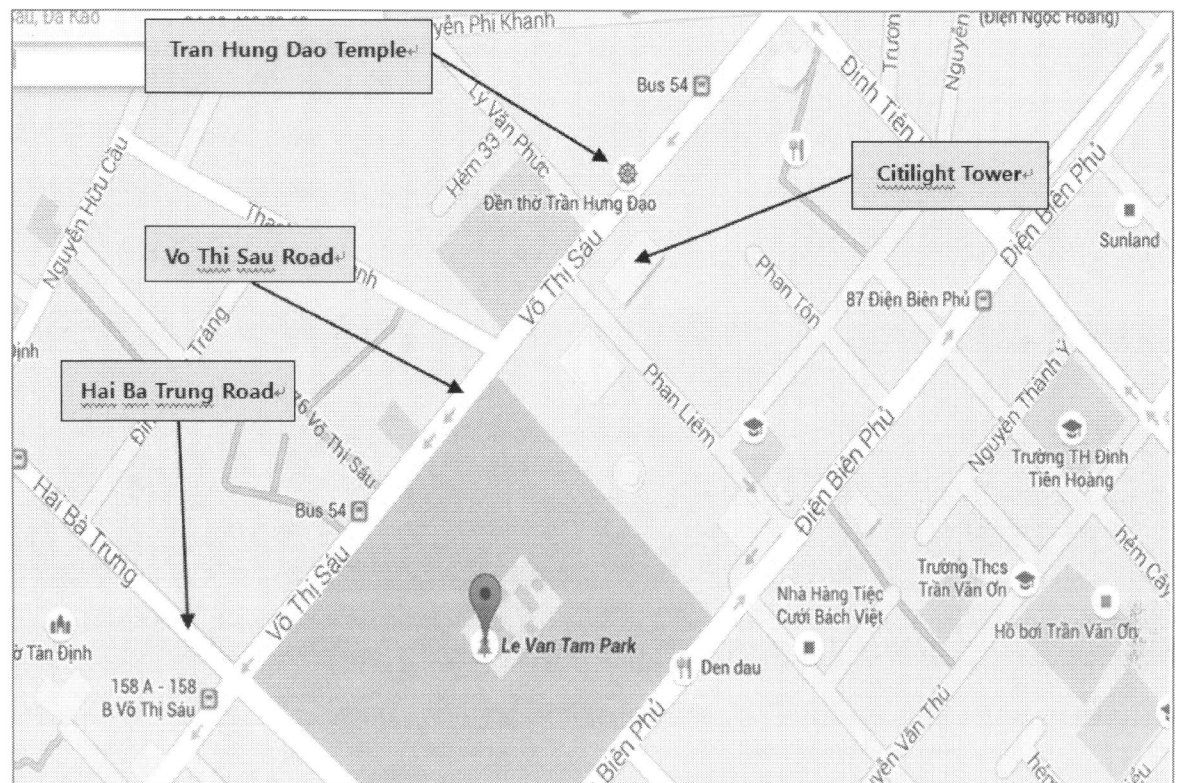

(When you go directly to the temple, turn to the right at the end of Le Van Tam Park. It means that you will change roads from "Hai Ba Trung Road" to "Vo Thi Sau Road". Then, you will meet Tran Hung Dao Temple around 200 meters ahead.)

("Citilight Tower" is standing on the street of "Vo Thi Sau Road". The temple is on the other side of the road. Now, let's go to the temple through the street of "Hai Ba Trung" from city center.)

(From Park Hyatt Hotel (right), you are looking back at the street of "Hai Ba Trung" on the left. "Hai Long 5 Hotel" is located between Park Hyatt Hotel and "Vietcombank Tower" standing high at the end of the road. Follow around 500 meters straight along the road as indicated by the yellow arrow on the photo. Then, you will meet "Le Van Tam Park" on your right.)

(You will meet "Kumho-Asiana Plaza (tall building) and Intercontinental Hotel (right) on the way to the park. They are standing on "Hai Ba Trung Road".)

(You are standing at a crossroads just before "Le Van Tam Park". The pink "NON SON" could be a milestone of the park.)

(Le Van Tam Park)

(There is a big parking lot for motorbikes.)

(The main entrance to Le Van Tam Park.)

(You will meet many people exercising various kinds of sports early in the morning.)

(Wide and beautiful "Le Van Tam Park".)

(Dancing)

(Badminton)

(Taichi.)

(And strolling. Now, let's go to "Tran Hung Dao Temple".)

(Come out of a gate from the park (left) and take the way to the right as indicated by the yellow arrow on the photo. It's "Vo Thi Sau Road". Then, you will meet "Citilight Tower" on your right in 3 minutes.)

(Citilight Tower. "Tran Hung Dao Temple" is on the other side of the road.)

(From "Citilight Tower", you are looking at the temple.)

(Tran Hung Dao Temple. Free admission.)

(Tran Hung Dao Temple. The legendary general is standing in front of the main shrine.)

(Main Shrine)

(Inside "Tran Hung Dao Temple".)

(The other side of the temple.)

(Main altar. "萬 古 江 山" means "No change forever". This is the end of your journey in Vietnam.)

I wish you have enjoyed a wonderful trip to Vietnam.

Made in the USA
Lexington, KY
27 August 2016